The Puzzle

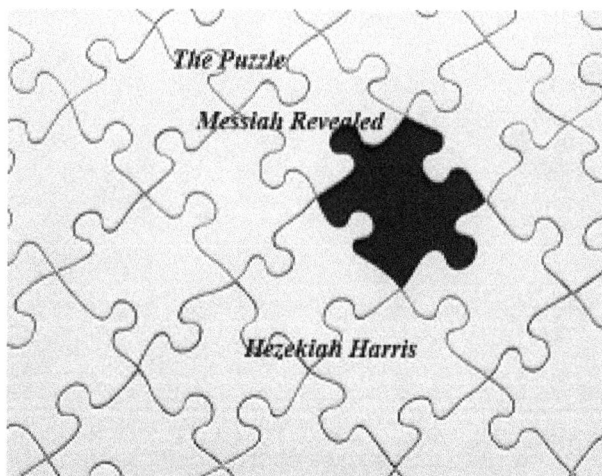

The Puzzle

Messiah Revealed

Hezekiah Harris

Messiah Revealed

Hezekiah Harris

ISBN: 978-0-578-51505-2

EMAIL: MessiahRevealed@Tutanota.com

CONTENTS

Preface

Open-mindedness is an attitude which is free from prejudice. It is difficult, however, for the average person not to be swayed or unduly dominated by the knowledge which he already has.

The one who is prejudiced hastily judges a case before all the evidence is in hand and, consequently, arrives at distorted conclusions. If a person has the willingness to see truth wherever it is and whatever it may be, he is willing to look at all sides of a given question and to examine carefully, honestly, and conscientiously what is presented by those holding opposite views. He has such an appreciation of truth that he is willing to renounce whatever error he may have held prior to his discovering some truth or fact previously unknown to him.

A willingness to renounce and repudiate error, held and cherished, is a rare trait of character. Having discovered some truth, a person must have the courage of his convictions to take his stand for the right regardless of the consequences. It takes moral boldness to accept truth publicly and to align oneself with the right, which is usually unpopular.

The one having the proper attitude toward truth must have an insatiable desire for it. He must want truth for the sake of truth, because it is right.

CHAPTER 1

"Is a Puzzlement"

...From the 1956 Broadway Play, "The King & I"

The Oxford dictionary defines a *puzzle* as a cause to feel confused because they cannot understand or make sense of something.

A question that is difficult to answer; a problem. A problem designed to test one's knowledge or patience. To confuse, cause doubt and uncertainty. To *puzzle over* and think hard about.

Other synonyms for *Puzzle* are: bewildered, perplexed, baffled, stumped, mystified, troubled, bemused, astonished, thrown off balance, and unable to understand.

Wikipedia tells us that a jigsaw puzzle is a tiling puzzle that requires the assembly of often oddly shaped interlocking and tessellating pieces. Each piece usually has a small part of a picture on it; when complete, a jigsaw puzzle produces a complete picture.

For over two-thousand years, the Jewish people have been attempting to solve the age old puzzle of who is their Messiah, and who is this figure in history known as Jesus ; Yeshua in Hebrew, which is translated as *"salvation"*, and the name I will use for him, going forward.

You will not find me sitting at the dining room table, alone or with family and friends, attempting to piece together a 500 piece jigsaw puzzle.

I was born in Brooklyn, N.Y., in the shadows of Ebbets Field, the home of the Brooklyn Dodgers baseball team before they moved to Los Angeles. My God was baseball, specifically, the Dodgers, but I would rather watch a replay of Don Larsen's Perfect Game victory over the Dodgers by the "Damn Yankees" (Damn Yankees is a musical comedy with a book by George Abbott and Douglass Wallop, music and lyrics by Richard Adler and Jerry Ross. The story is a modern retelling of the Faust legend set during the 1950s in Washington, D.C., during a time when the New York Yankees dominated Major League Baseball.) in the sixth game of the 1956 World Series, than work on a Jigsaw Puzzle.

For those of you who know nothing about baseball, what I'm trying to say is: I hate Jigsaw Puzzles.

I was really good at those 12 piece puzzles that had the shape of the puzzle piece outlined on the cardboard backing. Anything more complicated than that could be defined as any or all of the above stated definitions of a Puzzle...I like "baffled and troubled"

For those of you who actually enjoy the challenge of those 500 piece and larger jigsaw puzzles, and who have had success in completing them, I would like to offer you this challenge. You will have to use your imagination, common sense, and all of your right-brain expertise.

Here's the challenge: Placed in front of you is a 500-piece jigsaw puzzle.

I have removed the corner pieces, and the borders on all four sides.

I have also removed several pieces from the puzzle, and replaced them with several pieces from another puzzle. Finally, I have thrown away the box that the puzzle came in, and oh yes, the box cover as well, which means of course, that you have no picture of the completed puzzle!

How much time do you think you will need to complete that puzzle?

One day...One week... One month...A Year...Two-Thousand Years?

The complete puzzle, with all the missing pieces of the original puzzle included, all of the pieces that don't belong removed, all the corner pieces reinstated, all of the borders or foundations put in place, only then can the full picture come into clear focus. Only then can the identity of the Messiah be revealed. For all intents and purposes, this is the challenge that has faced the Jewish people for the last two-thousand years. In the natural, a puzzle that is virtually impossible to

11

solve. My goal in writing this book is twofold. First, to educate, assist and encourage the non-Jewish believer to share the "Good News" with Jewish people that God places in your path.

As Rabbi Saul, The Apostle Paul reminds us in Romans 1:16,"For I am not ashamed of the gospel of Messiah: for it is the power of God unto salvation to everyone that believes; to the Jew first, and also to the Greek".

Secondly, to put this book into the hands of as many Jewish people as possible so they can piece together this 2,000 year old puzzle, with the hope that they will receive the revelation of who their Messiah is.

Their Messiah is "The stone which the builders rejected has become the chief cornerstone". *Psalm 118:22*

CHAPTER 2

Restoring The Four Corner Pieces

Cornerstones, or corner pieces that have been removed, stand for difficulties which hinder the revelation of who Messiah is. They must be restored in order that King Messiah may be revealed. Of course, there are many; but there are four principal corner stones that must be put in place in order that Israel and the Jewish people may welcome her Messiah. Until these corners are restored with a true, scientific exposition of the Old Testament Scriptures, Israel cannot welcome Him; and until she pleads for His coming, He will not appear. The four missing corner pieces referred to above which must be restored are:

1.An understanding concerning the scriptural doctrine of the Triune nature of God; 2. the nature and person of King Messiah; 3.the entire redemptive career of Messiah; and 4. the time mentioned by the prophets when He would make His appearance in order to begin His world-wide redemptive work.

Since the Jewish people, as a rule, rejects the New Testament but holds to the Old, the truth on these four points must be given to him from the Scriptures which he accepts as genuine. Generally speaking, he believes that the five books of Moses are absolutely and inerrantly given by the Lord. The second division of the Old Testament, according to his idea, was not so completely inspired as were the books of Moses. These consist of the books beginning with Joshua and ending with II Kings, or the Prophets. In the Hebrew bible, the third division is called the Writings. According to Jewish opinion, this third section is less inspired than the second, which in turn is not so accurate as the five books of Moses. The reason the Rabbi's feels this way about the Old Testament is this: In Numbers 12 God said to Aaron and Miriam that He would speak to Moses face to face, but that to the prophets he would speak in a vision or a dream. The Rabbi's misunderstand this statement. To him it means that Moses was completely and inerrantly inspired, but that the prophets received and saw truth as a dream. Seldom are our dreams correct. According to his idea these latter, therefore, cannot be relied upon as one may depend upon the books of Moses. Of course, he misunderstands the meaning of this passage, but such is his opinion. In dealing with the Jewish people, one must recognize this fact and act accordingly. Whenever one is presenting any doctrine to a Jewish person, he must therefore point out the thought in the five books of Moses if possible, and then substantiate it by additional proof found in the other portions of the Old Testament. Of course, since the Jew does not believe the New Testament is God's Word, it is a mistake to bring proof from that portion of the Word until he has been taught what the truth is in those portions of the Word which he accepts as genuine and fully inspired.

The initial cornerstone in the Old Testament teaches that there is a Triune nature to God. The first verse of Genesis declares that "In the beginning God (Elohim) created"

In the beginning God created the heavens and the Earth. Genesis 1:1

"EL" is the singular for GOD, "ELOHIM" is the plural.

And God said, Let us make man in our image, after our likeness: and let them have dominion over the fish of the sea, and over the fowl of the air, and over the cattle, and over all the earth, and over every creeping thing that creepeth upon the earth. Genesis 1:26 Sounds like he wasn't alone!

At the same time the unity of the Divine Being is preserved in this very sentence by the use of the singular verb with the plural noun. Again the Triune nature is presupposed in Israel's great confession, Deuteronomy 6:4, "Hear, O Israel, The Lord our God is One (Echad- "The Lord a unity"- literal translation)

These are the words of Moses, stirring up the people to an attention to what he was about to say of this great and momentous article, the unity of God, to prevent their going into polytheism and idolatry.

These words form the beginning of what is termed the "Shema" ("Hear") in the Jewish Services, and belong to the daily morning and evening service. They may be called "the creed of the Jews."

This weighty text contains far more than a mere declaration of the unity of God as against polytheism; or of the sole authority of the revelation that He had made to Israel as against other pretended manifestations of His will and attributes. It asserts that the Lord God of Israel is absolutely God, and none other. He, and He alone, is Lord (YHVH) the absolute, uncaused God;

the One who had, by His election of them, made Himself known to Israel.

In modern Hebrew there is a term "Eshkol Echad", which translated literally means "One Cluster". Usually pertaining to fruit. Of course one cluster contains many grapes, or cherries, or whatever object one is talking about!

The Hebrew word for "one" is significant, viewed in the light of the fuller revelation of the New Testament. It stands, not for absolute unity, but for compound unity, to Unify, or a United One and is thus consistent with both the names of God used in this verse. The LORD emphasizes His oneness. Elohim (God) emphasizes His three persons.

In Hebrew, the word <u>"yachiyd"</u> is used to indicate <u>"one & only one"</u>. This word is translated into the English "only". It literally means <u>"only one"</u>, or <u>"solitary one"</u>

Here are three great examples of the difference between "Echad"(Compound Unity" and "Yachiyd"(Only One)

Gen 22:2 He said, "Take now your son , your <u>only (yachiyd)</u> son, whom you love , Isaac , and go to the land of Moriah , and offer him there as a burnt offering on one of the mountains of which I will tell you."

Proverbs 4:3 When I was a son to my father , Tender and the <u>only</u> (yachiyd) son in the sight of my mother ,

Zechariah 12:10 And I will pour upon the house of David, and upon the inhabitants of Jerusalem, the spirit of grace and of supplications: and they shall look upon me whom they have pierced, and they shall mourn for him, as one mourns for *his* only(yachyid) *son,* and shall be in bitterness for him, as one that is in bitterness for *his* firstborn. Not only does Zechariah give a great example of "yachyid", in this case, "only son", but delivers one of the greatest Messianic prophesies in all of the Old Testament bible. "And they shall look upon me whom they have pierced"…Wow, sounds like Yeshua to me!

By the way Zechariah lived around 500 BC.

From these examples we see that there is a plurality in the Godhead and at the same time these personalities constitute a unity. From other passages we learn that there are three: Father, Son, and Holy Spirit. In presenting the doctrine, therefore, of the Triune nature to the Jewish person, one must get his seed thought in the five books of Moses and then trace its development in the latter books of the Old Testament. By showing this, the scriptural teaching of Moses and the prophets concerning the Triune nature, one is restoring a most important corner to the puzzle.

The original word אלהים Elohim, God, is certainly the plural form of אל El, and has long been supposed, by the most eminently learned and pious men, to imply a plurality of Persons in the Divine nature. As this plurality appears in so many parts of the sacred writings to be confined to three Persons, hence the doctrine of the Triune Nature of God, which has formed a part of the creed of all those who have been deemed sound in the faith, from the earliest ages of Christianity. Nor are the Christians singular in receiving this doctrine, and in deriving it from the first words of Divine revelation. An eminent Jewish rabbi, Shimon ben Yochai, in his comment on the sixth section of Leviticus, has these remarkable words: "Come and see the mystery of the word Elohim; there are three degrees, and each degree by itself alone, and yet notwithstanding they are all one, and joined together in one, and are not divided from each other."

Shimon ben Yochai, also known by his acronym Rashbi, was a 2nd-century *tannaitic* sage in ancient Israel, said to be active after the destruction of the Second Temple in 70 CE. He was one of the most eminent disciples of Rabbi Akiva, and is pseudepigraphically attributed by many Orthodox Jews with the authorship of the Zohar, the chief work of Kabbalah.

In addition, important legal homilies called *Sifre* and *Mekhilta* are attributed to him. In the Mishnah, in which he is the fourth-most mentioned sage, he is often referred to as simply "Rabbi Shimon".

According to popular legend, he and his son, Eliezar ben Shimon, were noted Kabbalists. Both figures are held in unique reverence by kabbalistic tradition. They were buried in the same tomb in Meron, Israel, which is visited by thousands year round.

The second cornerstone that must be restored in order that Israel's Messiah may be revealed, is the misconception concerning the nature and person of King Messiah. The Jewish person looks at the historical record in Samuel, Kings, and Chronicles, and reads that such men as Saul, David, Solomon, and the kings of Judah were called God's Messiahs. They realize that these men were born by natural generation, that they served their day and generation, and that many of them fell into gross errors and mistakes, and finally died. From these facts he formulates his idea of King Messiah, concluding that he is but another man who is born by natural generation, that he will be a great genius beyond doubt, and that He will eventually restore Israel to her position as head of the nations. Thus Messiah, to the modern Jew, is simply a great military and political genius. Of a superhuman Messiah, who is one of the persons of the Godhead, entering the world by miraculous conception and virgin birth, he knows absolutely nothing. He does not understand the teaching of his own Scriptures concerning the nature of King Messiah. He is indeed shocked when he is told by Christians that Yeshua was his Messiah because He was begotten by the Holy Spirit and conceived and brought forth by the Virgin Mary. The New Testament records seem to him to be absolutely contrary to the Old Testament and to reason; therefore, the message of the New Testament is by him, rejected.

In order to restore this cornerstone, the intelligent earnest messenger must show first from Moses and then from the writings of the prophets what they said concerning the supernatural character of King Messiah and His Virgin birth. Having shown from Moses and the prophets that He is God in human form, the messenger to Israel is ready to give him the teaching of the New Testament.

A good example from the first five books (The Torah) are Genesis 3:15 *"And I will put enmity between thee and the woman, and between thy seed and her seed; it shall bruise thy head, and thou shalt bruise his heel"*.

A prediction that a seed of a women shall deal a crushing blow to the great adversary of the human race. A prediction which to this day, continues to baffle Jewish scholars.

Isaiah 7:14 *"Therefore the Lord himself shall give you a sign(Ot); Behold, a virgin(Alma) shall conceive, and bear a son, and shall call his name Immanuel"* *(Which translated mean "God with Us")* In Hebrew *emanu el*

Our Rabbis would tell us that the Hebrew word "Alma" means young maiden and not virgin. What they failed to tell us is that in the Septuagint, (the Greek translation of the Hebrew text compiled by 70 Rabbi's), completed around 50 B.C. for the Jewish people of the world returning to Israel after the exile who had virtually lost the ability to understand the Hebrew text,) was translated as "Virgin". The word those Rabbis used was "Parthenos", which only has one meaning-Virgin! What is just as important, though, is the Hebrew word אות (ot), meaning sign. A study of the word in other passages clearly indicate that אות

means a genuine miracle, the inevitable conclusion demanded by all the facts that the prediction for tells the miraculous conception and virgin birth of the child here promised.

Isaiah 9:6 *"For unto us a child is born, unto us a son is given: and the government shall be upon his shoulder: and his name shall be called Wonderful, Counsellor, The mighty God, The everlasting Father, The Prince of Peace".Of the increase of His government and peace there will be no end,   upon the throne of David and over His kingdom, To order it and establish it with judgment and justice from that time forward, even forever. The zeal of the LORD of hosts will perform this .*

Simply stated, when the idea of the verses are blended, the complete thought is that God promises to give his Son in the form of a child to mount the throne of David and to establish peace in Israel. The prophet Isaiah spoke of this (Isaiah 9:6) around 750 B.C. In order for this one to accomplish the work of subjecting Israel's foes, he must be what these words imply, namely, the Mighty God, Everlasting Father, and The Prince of Peace.

This prophesy is so powerful and revealing, that the Jewish Publication Society in many early versions of their English edition of the Old Testament, chose to substitute the "Hebrew Transliteration" in place of 'Wonderful", Counsellor", "Mighty God", Everlasting Father", "Prince Of Peace", knowing that most American Jews don't speak a lick of Hebrew and would not understand what Isaiah is trying to tell us. It reads …"and his name shall be called "Pele, Yoets, El Gibbor, Avi Ad, Sar-Shalom"

Psalm 2:1 Why do the heathen rage, and the people imagine a vain thing?

Psa 2:2 The kings of the earth set themselves, and the rulers take counsel together, against the LORD, and against his anointed, *saying,*

Psa 2:3 Let us break their bands asunder, and cast away their cords from us.

Psa 2:4 He that sitteth in the heavens shall laugh: the Lord shall have them in derision.

Psa 2:5 Then shall he speak unto them in his wrath, and vex them in his sore displeasure.

Psa 2:6 Yet have I set my king upon my holy hill of Zion.

Psa 2:7 I will declare the decree: the LORD hath said unto me, Thou *art* my Son; this day have I begotten thee.

Psa 2:8 Ask of me, and I shall give *thee* the heathen *for* thine inheritance, and the uttermost parts of the earth *for* thy possession.

Psa 2:9 Thou shalt break them with a rod of iron; thou shalt dash them in pieces like a potter's vessel.

Psa 2:10 Be wise now therefore, O ye kings: be instructed, ye judges of the earth.

Psa 2:11 Serve the LORD with fear, and rejoice with trembling.

Psa 2:12 Kiss the Son, lest he be angry, and ye perish *from* the way, when his wrath is kindled but a little. Blessed *are* all they that put their trust in him.

The historical background of this passage demand the identification of the Messiah as the King who is to be installed as the world Ruler. God addresses him as "thou art my son", and on that basis, states that the nations of the earth are to be his inheritance. From the last section of the psalm it is evident that the Son is put on an equality with God and appeals for the rulers to serve the Lord and to Kiss the Son

Micah 5:2 But thou, Bethlehem Ephratah, *though* thou be little among the thousands of Judah, *yet* out of thee shall he come forth unto me *that is* to be ruler in Israel; whose goings forth *have been* from of old, from everlasting.(Olam)

The key point the Prophet Micah is making is this ruler in Israel is the "eternal" ruler, the Hebrew "olam" meaning eternal or perpetual.

Almost everyone has heard that Jesus, Yeshua, was born in Bethlehem!

These are all sound proof texts that the Messiah, Yeshua, is God in human form.

 "Theophanies", biblical accounts of appearances of God in the form of a man are all great examples in the Old Testament of the ability of God to show up looking like a man, just like he did in the first century.

If you haven't seen the 1977 classic movie "Oh,God!", starring George Burns and John Denver, you missed one of the funniest movies that Hollywood has ever produced.

Denver plays an assistant manager of a supermarket who is visited throughout the movie by God, played by George Burns.

God shows up, looking like a man, an older man, I must say, who comes up with the classic line on his first appearance to Denver, "not what you expected?"

Here is a very large and important puzzle piece that must be restored.

Jewish people know that we believe that Yeshua is God in human form. Not only is he the Messiah- he is God. That thought is incomprehensible to Jewish thinking. In addition to that, first century Jews didn't recognize Yeshua as the Messiah, let alone God, because "it's not what they were expecting". That thought process has gone on for two-thousand years...He's not who they were looking for.

Their typical retort is: If Jesus was the Messiah, then why isn't there world peace? How can a person be God?

Jewish people, if they have read the Tenach (Old Testament) at all, have only read the Torah, the first five books, if even that. They are unfamiliar with Old Testament prophesies regarding the Messiah, and unfamiliar with bible theophanies, appearances of God in the form of a man, that show up in the Old Testament.

Each Theophany is a puzzle piece that
will continue to complete the
picture and reveal the Jewish
Messiah.

Following are four well-known bible
stories that describe amazing
encounters.

Jacob Wrestles with God

Genesis 32:22 And he rose up that
night, and took his two wives, and his
two women servants, and his eleven
sons, and passed over the ford
Jabbok.

Gen 32:23 And he took them, and sent
them over the brook, and sent over
that he had.

Gen 32:24 And Jacob was left alone;
and there wrestled a man with him
until the breaking of the day.

Gen 32:25 And when he saw that he
prevailed not against him, he touched
the hollow of his thigh; and the hollow
of Jacob's thigh was out of joint, as he

wrestled with him.

Gen 32:26 And he said, Let me go, for the day breaketh. And he said, I will not let thee go, except thou bless me.

Gen 32:27 And he said unto him, What *is* thy name? And he said, Jacob.

Gen 32:28 And he said, Thy name shall be called no more Jacob, but Israel: for as a prince hast thou power with God and with men, and hast prevailed.

Gen 32:29 And Jacob asked *him,* and said, Tell *me,* I pray thee, thy name. And he said, Wherefore *is* it *that* thou dost ask after my name? And he blessed him there.

Gen 32:30 And Jacob called the name of the place Peniel: for I have seen God face to face, and my life is preserved.

Gen 32:31 And as he passed over Peniel the sun rose upon him, and he halted upon his thigh.

Gen 32:32 Therefore the children of Israel eat not *of* the sinew which shrank, which *is* upon the hollow of the thigh, unto this day: because he touched the hollow of Jacob's thigh in the sinew that shrank.

So we have in the very first book of the Torah, Genesis, a perfect example of God showing up in the form of a man!

The next one is one of my favorites. The appearance of God to the parents of Samson in the thirteenth chapter of the book of Judges.

Judges 13:1 And the children of Israel again did that which was evil in the sight of the LORD; and the LORD delivered them into the hand of the Philistines forty years.

Jdg 13:2 And there was a certain man of Zorah, of the family of the Danites, whose name was Manoah; and his wife was barren, and bore not.

Jdg 13:3 And the angel of the LORD appeared unto the woman, and said unto her: 'Behold now, thou art barren, and hast not borne; but thou shalt conceive, and bear a son.

Jdg 13:4 Now therefore beware, I pray thee, and drink no wine nor strong drink, and eat not any unclean thing.

Jdg 13:5 For, lo, thou shalt conceive, and bear a son; and no razor shall come upon his head; for the child shall be a Nazirite unto God from the womb; and he shall begin to save Israel out of the hand of the Philistines.'

Jdg 13:6 Then the woman came and told her husband, saying: 'A man of God came unto me, and his countenance was like the countenance of the angel of God, very terrible; and I asked him not whence he was, neither told he me his name;

Jdg 13:7 but he said unto me: Behold, thou shalt conceive, and bear a son; and now drink no wine nor strong drink, and eat not any unclean thing; for the child shall be a Nazirite unto God from the womb to the day of his death.'

Jdg 13:8 Then Manoah entreated the LORD, and said: 'Oh, LORD, I pray Thee, let the man of God whom Thou didst send come again unto us, and teach us what we shall do unto the child that shall be born.'

Jdg 13:9 And God hearkened to the voice of Manoah; and the angel of God came again unto the woman as she sat in the field; but Manoah her husband was not with her.

Jdg 13:10 And the woman made haste, and ran, and told her husband, and said unto him: 'Behold, the man hath appeared unto me, that came unto me that day.'

Jdg 13:11 And Manoah arose, and went after his wife, and came to the man, and said unto him: 'Art thou the man that spokest unto the woman?' And he said: 'I am.'

Jdg 13:12 And Manoah said: 'Now when thy word cometh to pass, what shall be the rule for the child, and what shall be done with him?'

Jdg 13:13 And the angel of the LORD said unto Manoah: 'Of all that I said unto the woman let her beware.

Jdg 13:14 She may not eat of anything that cometh of the grapevine, neither let her drink wine or strong drink, nor eat any unclean thing; all that I commanded her let her observe.'

Jdg 13:15 And Manoah said unto the angel of the LORD: 'I pray thee, let us detain thee, that we may make ready a kid for thee.'

Jdg 13:16 And the angel of the LORD said unto Manoah: 'Though thou detain me, I will not eat of thy bread; and if thou wilt make ready a burnt-offering, thou must offer it unto the LORD.' For Manoah knew not that he was the angel of the LORD.

Jdg 13:17 And Manoah said unto the angel of the LORD: 'What is thy name, that when thy words come to pass we may do thee honor?'

Jdg 13:18 And the angel of the LORD

said unto him: 'Wherefore asked thou after my name, seeing it is *wonderful*?' (Pele in Hebrew, as in Isaiah 9:6)

Jdg 13:19 So Manoah took the kid with the meal-offering, and offered it upon the rock unto the LORD; and the angel did wondrously, and Manoah and his wife looked on.

Jdg 13:20 For it came to pass, when the flame went up toward heaven from off the altar, that the angel of the LORD ascended in the flame of the altar; and Manoah and his wife looked on; and they fell on their faces to the ground.

Jdg 13:21 But the angel of the LORD did no more appear to Manoah or to his wife. Then Manoah knew that he was the angel of the LORD.

Jdg 13:22 And Manoah said unto his wife: 'We shall surely die, because we have seen God.'

Jdg 13:23 But his wife said unto him: 'If the LORD were pleased to kill us, He would not have received a burnt-offering and a meal- offering at our hand, neither would He have shown us all these things, nor would at this time have told such things as these.'

Jdg 13:24 And the woman bore a son, and called his name Samson; and the child grew, and the LORD blessed him.

Jdg 13:25 And the spirit of the LORD began to move him in Mahaneh-dan, between Zorah and Eshtaol.

The mysterious guest is referred to as a MAN and GOD. The text is clear that the mystery man is BOTH!

Listed below are the first 21 verses of Genesis 18.

Genesis 18:1 And the LORD appeared unto him by the terebinths of Mamre, as he sat in the tent door in the heat of the day;

Gen 18:2 and he lifted up his eyes and looked, and, lo, three men stood over against him; and when he saw them, he ran to meet them from the tent door, and bowed down to the earth,

Gen 18:3 and said: 'My lord, if now I have found favour in thy sight, pass not away, I pray thee, from thy servant.

Gen 18:4 Let now a little water be fetched, and wash your feet, and recline yourselves under the tree.

Gen 18:5 And I will fetch a morsel of bread, and stay ye your heart; after that ye shall pass on; forasmuch as ye are come to your servant.' And they said: 'So do, as thou hast said.'

Gen 18:6 And Abraham hastened into the tent unto Sarah, and said: 'Make ready quickly three measures of fine meal, knead it, and make cakes.'

Gen 18:7 And Abraham ran unto the herd, and fetched a calf tender and good, and gave it unto the servant; and he hastened to dress it.

Gen 18:8 And he took curd, and milk, and the calf which he had dressed, and set it before them; and he stood by them under the tree, and they did eat.

Gen 18:9 And they said unto him: 'Where is Sarah thy wife?' And he said: 'Behold, in the tent.'

Gen 18:10 And He said: 'I will certainly return unto thee when the season cometh round; and, lo, Sarah thy wife shall have a son.' And Sarah heard in the tent door, which was behind him. -

Gen 18:11 Now Abraham and Sarah were old, and well stricken in age; it had ceased to be with Sarah after the manner of women. -

Gen 18:12 And Sarah laughed within herself, saying: 'After I am waxed old shall I have pleasure, my lord being old also?'

Gen 18:13 And the LORD said unto Abraham: 'Wherefore did Sarah laugh, saying: Shall I of a surety bear a child, who am old?

Gen 18:14 Is anything too hard for the LORD. At the set time I will return unto thee, when the season cometh round, and Sarah shall have a son.'

Gen 18:15 Then Sarah denied, saying: 'I laughed not'; for she was afraid. And He said: 'Nay; but thou didst laugh.'

Gen 18:16 And the men rose up from thence, and looked out toward Sodom; and Abraham went with them to bring them on the way.

Gen 18:17 And the LORD said: 'Shall I hide from Abraham that which I am doing;

Gen 18:18 seeing that Abraham shall surely become a great and mighty nation, and all the nations of the earth shall be blessed in him?

Gen 18:19 For I have known him, to the end that he may command his children and his household after him, that they may keep the way of the LORD, to do righteousness and justice; to the end that the LORD may bring upon Abraham that which He hath spoken of him.'

Gen 18:20 And the LORD said:

'Verily, the cry of Sodom and Gomorrah is great, and, verily, their sin is exceeding grievous.

Gen 18:21 I will go down now, and see whether they have done altogether according to the cry of it, which is come unto Me; and if not, I will know.'

Asher Intrater in his book, "Who Ate Lunch With Abraham" describes the encounter.

"Scholars and Rabbinic commentators go to great lengths to explain that this chapter cannot be taken in a literal or plain sense meaning. Yet the text is EXPLICIT and quite "PHYSICAL" in the detail of its description.."

"The staggering and inescapable truth is that the Lord (YHVH) himself comes to visit Abraham in the form of a human being. They have lunch and discuss together a number of important issues."

"So here we have it…Abraham meets with God manifest in human bodily form. If God appeared to Abraham in human form, then the foundational objection to the divinity of Yeshua disappears."

"One can argue that he does not see the figure in Genesis 18 as Yeshua. However, it cannot be reasonably argued that the Genesis 18 text does not describe an appearance of the Lord(YHVH) in human bodily form."

"THAT APPEARANCE OF GOD IN A HUMAN FORM TO ABRAHAM REMOVES THE MOST FUNDAMENTAL REASON IN JEWISH THINKING FOR NOT BELIEVING IN YESHUA."

"In the New Covenant, John Chapter 8, specifically makes the claim that the

One who visited Abraham was
Yeshua."

John 8:56 Your father Abraham
    rejoiced to see my day; and he saw
    it, and was glad.

John 8:57 The Jews therefore said
    unto him, Thou art not yet fifty
    years old, and hast thou seen
    Abraham?

John 8:58 Yeshua said unto them,
    Verily, verily, I say unto you,
    Before Abraham was born, I am.

John 8:59 They took up stones
    therefore to cast at him: but Yeshua
    hid himself, and went out of the
    temple.

Two of the three "theophanies" are
    from the Torah. As mentioned in an
    earlier chapter, the most revered

portion of the Tenach(Old Testament) to the Jewish people!

I must include two more from the Book of Daniel. I have saved the best for last.

The text is from the Book of Daniel, verses 13-14

The Son of Man Is Given Dominion

Dan 7:13 I saw in the night visions, and, behold, *one* like the Son of man came with the clouds of heaven, and came to the Ancient of days, and they brought him near before him.

Dan 7:14 And there was given him dominion, and glory, and a kingdom, that all people, nations, and languages, should serve him: his dominion *is* an everlasting dominion, which shall not pass away, and his kingdom *that* which shall not be destroyed.

The ancient Jewish writing, the Book of Zohar it says:

"in the times of the Messiah, Israel shall be one people, to the Lord, and he shall make them one nation in the earth, and they shall rule above and below; as it is written, "behold, one like the Son of man came with the clouds of heaven"; this is the King Messiah of whom it is written, "and in the days of these kings shall the God of heaven, set up a kingdom which shall never be destroyed".

Daniel 3:25 "Look!" he answered, "I see four men loose, walking in the midst of the fire; and they are not hurt, and the form of the fourth is like the Son of God." I need to repeat the last eight words...and the form of the fourth is like the Son Of God!

This of course is the famous story of Daniel's friends, Shadrach, Meshach, and Abednego(Hananiah, Mishael, and Azariah) thrown into the fiery furnace for not bowing down to the Image.

The term "Son of Man" is meant to imply that his appearance is that of a regular looking person. In modern Hebrew, the term Ben Adam (literally "Son of Man")is used all the time to describe a person...just a regular looking guy.

Yeshua describes himself as "The Son Of Man" many times throughout the New Testament

Critical pieces of the puzzle have now been put in place.

There are literally scores of 'appearances" of the Lord (YHVH) to individuals throughout the Tenach. Appearances to David, Solomon, Isaac, and many of the prophets. In addition, most bible scholars would agree that the Angel Of The Lord and The Word Of The Lord(Memra), by definition, are the exact representation of God, showing up in the form of a man. When you add up all those appearances, the total reaches triple digits.

The modern Jew thinks that Messiah, as stated before, is simply a man who is born by natural generation, who will serve his day and generation and pass on. Of the redemptive career of King Messiah as outlined by Moses and the prophets, consisting of the first coming when He is rejected, His ascension to the right hand of the throne of God, and His eventual return when Israel accepts Him, the Jewish person knows absolutely nothing. To affirm that Yeshua was the Messiah who fulfilled the predictions concerning His first coming, who after His resurrection returned to heaven, and who will come again to fulfill the glorious predictions of the prophets, seems to the Jew to be but an effort on the part of Christians to build up a case to bolster the claims for Yeshua, which they believe are false. It is therefore necessary for one, beginning with Moses, to show what the Old Testament foretells concerning the entire redemptive work of King Messiah. God through Moses and the prophets did give us a blueprint of the entire career of Messiah: His first coming, His session at the right hand of God, His return and rule upon earth.

The addition of the redemptive work of King Messiah is the restoring of the third great corner piece.

Isa 48:17 states: Thus saith the LORD, thy Redeemer, the Holy One of Israel: I am the LORD thy God, who teacheth thee for thy profit, who leadeth thee by the way that thou shouldest go.
The need for a Redeemer is clearly portrayed in the fifty-ninth chapter of Isaiah where it says in verse 2: But

your iniquities have separated between you and your God, and your sins have hid His face from you, that He will not hear.

Verse 9: Therefore is justice far from us, neither doth righteousness overtake us; we look for light, but behold darkness, for brightness, but we walk in gloom.

Verse 11: We all growl like bears, and mourn sore like doves; we look for right, but there is none; for salvation, but it is far off from us.

Verse 12: For our transgressions are multiplied before Thee, and our sins testify against us; for our transgressions are present to us, and as for our iniquities, we know them:

Because of our sins and iniquities, God has hidden his face from us.

Leviticus 17:11 states, For the life of the flesh *is* in the blood: and I have given it to you upon the altar to make an atonement for your souls: for it *is* the blood *that* maketh an atonement

54

for the soul.

According to the Scriptures, sin must be paid for. When Yeshua died, he suffered as a substitute in the place of and on behalf of fallen humanity. Messiah's death made it possible for men and women to be declared righteous, based on their faith in Him. Messiah's death was not merely a statement against evil or an expression of love, but a payment that satisfied God's demand.

God instituted the sacrificial system as a way of Israel atoning for its sins as depicted throughout the book of Leviticus.

As the High Priest laid one hand on the animal that was offered up, and the other hand on the head of the "sinner", the shed blood of the sacrificial animal, fulfilled the requirement of Leviticus 17:11. The sin passed from the man to the animal who was the substitute atonement.

This was just a type, a picture of what

was to follow through the death and resurrection of the Messiah, Yeshua.

Many Jewish people don't even know the main purpose of the Temple that stood in Jerusalem for so many years. Nor do they understand why a man named Jesus was crucified on a cross, and all of a sudden everyone thinks he's God!

They don't realize that the Last Supper was a Passover Seder, and that Yeshua was the Passover lamb, the Holy One of Israel, the Redeemer, who's vicarious atonement was for all of mankind .

Here is the greatest proof text in the Tenach(Old Testament).

ISAIAH 53- THE FORBIDDEN CHAPTER

This remarkable prophesy of the "suffering Messiah" was written 700 years before the time of Yeshua. It reads like a historical summary of the Gospel narrative. One commentator has said "it reads as if it had been written beneath the cross of Golgotha"

Unfortunately, the chapter division comes at the wrong place. It should begin with Isaiah 52:13, which starts with the words "BEHOLD MY SERVANT"…and that is the subject of the entire section. The graphic portrayal of The Suffering Messiah… "Jehovah's Servant"

LET'S READ IT THROUGH

Isaiah 52:13 Behold, my servant shall deal prudently, he shall be exalted and extolled, and be very high.

Isa 52:14 As many were astonished at thee; his visage was so marred more than any man, and his form more than the sons of men:

Isa 52:15 So shall he sprinkle many nations; the kings shall shut their mouths at him: for *that* which had not been told them shall they see; and *that* which they had not heard shall they consider.

Isa 53:1 Who hath believed our report? and to whom is the arm of the LORD revealed?

Isa 53:2 For he shall grow up before him as a tender plant, and as a root out of a dry ground: he hath no form nor comeliness; and when we shall see him, *there is* no beauty that we should desire him.

Isa 53:3 He is despised and rejected of men; a man of sorrows, and acquainted with grief: and we hid as it were *our* faces from him; he was despised, and we esteemed him not.

Isa 53:4 Surely he hath borne our griefs, and carried our sorrows: yet we did esteem him stricken, smitten of God, and afflicted.

Isa 53:5 But he *was* <u>wounded for our transgressions,</u> *he was* <u>bruised for our iniquities:</u> the chastisement of our peace *was* upon him; and with his stripes we are healed.

Isa 53:6 All we like sheep have gone astray; we have turned everyone to his own way; and <u>the LORD hath laid on him the iniquity of us all.</u>

Isa 53:7 He was oppressed, and he was afflicted, yet he opened not his mouth: he is brought as a lamb to the slaughter, and as a sheep before her shearers is dumb, so he openeth not his mouth.

Isa 53:8 He was taken from prison and from judgment: and who shall declare his generation? for he was cut off out of the land of the living:

<u>for the transgression of my people
was he stricken.</u>

Isa 53:9 And he made his grave with
the wicked, and with the rich in his
death; because he had done no
violence, neither *was any* deceit in
his mouth.

Isa 53:10 Yet it pleased the LORD to
bruise him; he hath put *him* to
grief: when <u>thou shalt make his soul
an offering for sin,</u> he shall see *his*
seed, he shall prolong *his* days, and
the pleasure of the LORD shall
prosper in his hand.

Isa 53:11 He shall see of the travail of
his soul, *and* shall be satisfied: by
his knowledge shall my righteous
servant justify many; <u>for he shall
bear their iniquities.</u>

Isa 53:12 Therefore will I divide him *a
portion* with the great, and he shall

divide the spoil with the strong; because he hath poured out his soul unto death: and he was numbered with the transgressors; and <u>he bare the sin of many, and made intercession for the transgressors.</u>

Despite what seems so clear to us, there are relatively few believers among Messiah's own people!!

In Pesiqta Rabbati 37:1 a remarkable Midrash, an ancient rabbinic commentary of portions of the Hebrew Scriptures, records a conversation between the Patriarchs and Messiah:

"In the latter days, the Fathers (Abraham, Isaac and Jacob) will stand up in the month of Nissan(at the Passover)and say, 'Ephraim the Messiah, our righteousness, though we are the Fathers, yet Thou art better than we, because Thou hast borne all the sins of our sons, and hard and evil measure has passed on to Thee, such as has not been passed either upon those before, or those after. Messiah tells them that he did this for their sakes and the sakes of their children. To this they reply: Ephraim the Messiah, our righteousness, be Thou reconciled to us, because Thou have reconciled Thy maker to us.

The fourth corner piece that must be restored is the Jewish misconception concerning the time when Messiah was scheduled by the prophets to come the first time. One outstanding rabbi has said that Christianity and Judaism are diametrically opposed and that they can never be reconciled. In explaining his position he declared that the fundamental tenets of each of these religious faiths are as far apart as the poles. "The Jew," he asserted, "believes that Messiah has never come." The Christian affirms that that He was born two thousand years ago. In other words, the Christian believes with all his being that which the Jew denies with equal emphasis. If the Messiah has come, the Christians are right in their contention. If He has never made his appearance, the Jew is correct in adhering to Moses and the prophets and in rejecting Christianity. It is a matter of prime importance that the messenger to Israel must be able to show when Moses and the prophets said that Messiah would come. In other words, he must know the Old Testament teaching concerning chronology, for, according to the inspired men of God, Messiah was to come at a certain time. Moses drew the bare sketch of His redemptive career, but the details were filled in by the latter prophets. It was left to Daniel to show the very year when he would be "cut off". There were those in Israel at the time of Yeshua who believed the prophets, and who were thoroughly convinced that they were living in the time when Messiah would be born; hence, they were alert to discover any sign pointing in that direction. They were not disappointed. The Jew today has misread his Scriptures with reference to the time for Messiah's first appearance. To show the chronological scheme in the Old Testament, proving to him exactly when Messiah was to appear the first time, is therefore to restore the fourth and last great missing corner piece, in order that Messiah may come to Israel and bring the longed-for redemption.

To fully appreciate the remarkable significance of the following passages of scripture, it is essential to realize that the Book of Daniel, as part of the

Old Testament, was translated into Greek prior to 270 BC, almost three centuries before Messiah was born. This is a well-established fact of secular history.

It is recorded in the Scriptures that Daniel (originally deported as a teenager, though now near the end of the Babylonian captivity) was reading in the Book of Jeremiah and made a discovery. He understood that the seventy years of servitude were almost over and he began to pray for his people. The Angel Gabriel interrupted Daniel's prayer and gave him a four-verse prophecy that is unquestionably the most remarkable passage in the entire Bible: Daniel 9:24-27.

These four verses include the following segments:

9:24 The Scope of the Entire Prophecy;
9:25 The 69 Weeks;

9:26 An Interval between the 69th and 70th Week;
9:27 The 70th Week.

The Scope

"Seventy weeks are determined upon thy people and upon thy holy city, to finish the transgression, and to make an end of sins, and to make reconciliation for iniquity, and to bring in everlasting righteousness, and to seal up the vision and prophecy, and to anoint the most Holy Place (Daniel 9:24)."

The idiom of a "week" of years was common in Israel as a "sabbath for the land," in which the land was to lie fallow every seventh year. It was their failure to obey these laws that led to God sending them into captivity under the Babylonians. Note that the focus of this passage is upon "thy people and upon thy holy city," that is, upon Israel and Jerusalem (it is not directed to the Church). The scope of this prophecy includes a broad list of things which clearly have yet to be completed.

The First 69 Weeks

A very specific prediction occurs in verse 25:

"Know therefore and understand, that from the going forth of the commandment to restore and to build Jerusalem unto the Messiah the Prince shall be seven weeks, and threescore and two weeks: the street shall be built again, and the wall, even in troublous times."

This includes a mathematical prophecy. The Jewish (and Babylonian) calendars used a 360-day year; 69 weeks of 360-day years totals 173,880 days. In effect, Gabriel told Daniel that the interval between the commandment to rebuild Jerusalem until the presentation of the Messiah

as King would be 173,880 days. The
"Messiah the Prince" in the King
James translation is actually the
Meshiach Nagid, "The Messiah the
King." (Nagid is first used of King
Saul.)

The commandment to restore and
build Jerusalem was given by
Artaxerxes Longimanus on March 14,
445 BC. (The emphasis in the verse on
"the street" and "the wall" was to
avoid confusion with other earlier
mandates confined to rebuilding the
Temple.)

During the ministry of Yeshua there
were several occasions in which the
people attempted to promote Him as
king, but He carefully avoided it
saying: "My hour is not yet come"
Then, one day, He meticulously
arranges it. On this particular day
(Palm Sunday) He rode into the city of
Jerusalem riding on a donkey,
deliberately fulfilling a prophecy by

Zechariah that the Messiah would present Himself as king in just that way:

"Rejoice greatly, O daughter of Zion; shout, O daughter of Jerusalem: behold, thy King cometh unto thee: he is just, and having salvation; lowly, and riding upon an ass, and upon a colt the foal of an ass (Zechariah 9:9)."

Whenever we might easily miss the significance of what was going on, the Pharisees come to our rescue. They felt that the overzealous crowd was blaspheming, proclaiming Yeshua as the Messiah the King. However, Yeshua says: *"I tell you that, if these should hold their peace, the stones would immediately cry out (Luke 19:40)."*

This is the only occasion that Yeshua presented Himself as King. It occurred on April 6, 32 AD. When we examine the period between March 14, 445 BC and April 6, 32 AD, and correct for leap years, we discover that it is 173,880 days exactly, to the very day!

The Interval

There appears to be a gap between the 69th week (verse 25) and the 70th week (verse 27):

"And after threescore and two weeks shall Messiah be cut off, but not for himself: and the people of the prince that shall come shall destroy the city and the sanctuary; and the end thereof shall be with a flood, and unto the end of the war desolations are determined (Daniel 9:26)."

The sixty-two "weeks" follow the initial seven, so verse 26 deals with events after 69th week, but before the 70th. These events include the Messiah being killed and the city and sanctuary being destroyed.

As Yeshua approached the city on the donkey, He also predicted the destruction of Jerusalem:

"For the days shall come upon thee, that thine enemies shall cast a trench about thee, and compass thee round, and keep thee in on every side, And shall lay thee even with the ground, and thy children within thee; and they shall not leave in thee one stone upon another; because thou knewest not the time of thy visitation (Luke 19:43-44)."

The Messiah was, of course, executed at the Crucifixion. The city and the sanctuary were destroyed 38 years later when the Roman legions under Titus Vespasian leveled the city of Jerusalem in AD 70, precisely as Daniel and Yeshua had predicted. In fact, as one carefully examines Yeshua's specific words, it appears that He held them accountable to know this astonishing prophecy in Daniel 9: "because thou knewest not the time of thy visitation."

The 70th Week

There is a remaining seven-year period yet to be fulfilled. This period is the most documented period in the entire Bible. The Book of Revelation, Chapters 6 through 19, is essentially a detailing of that climactic period.

We are being plunged into a period of time about which the Bible says more than it does about any other period in human history - including the time when Yeshua walked the shores of the Sea of Galilee or climbed the mountains of Judea. Examine the scriptures for yourself and you will discover that the Bible is as relevant and accurate today as it was two thousand years ago.

Adam Clarke (1760 or 1762 - 1832) was a British Methodist theologian and Biblical scholar. He is chiefly remembered for writing a *commentary* on the entire bible that took 40 years, and is considered one of the most important commentaries ever written.

Following, is his commentary on the Daniel 9 prophesy:

Most learned men agree that the death of Messiah happened at the Passover in the month Nisan, in the four thousand seven hundred and forty-sixth year of the Julian period. Four hundred and ninety years, reckoned back from the above year, leads us directly to the month Nisan in the four thousand two hundred and fifty-sixth year of the same period; the very month and year in which Ezra had his commission from Artaxerxes Longimanus, king of Persia, (see Ezra 7:9), to restore and rebuild Jerusalem. See the commission in Ezra 7:11-26.

A. The 1990 edition of the Encyclopedia Britannica states that Artaxerxes ascended to the throne of the Medo-Persian empire in July 465 B.C.E.

The day of the decree to restore and rebuild Jerusalem was twenty (20) years after he took office, <u>2nd Chapter of Nehemiah</u>, putting that date at 445 B.C.E.

69 "years of weeks" x 7 is 483 years.

If you add 483 years to 445 B.C, your arrive at 38 A.D.

The difference between 176,295 days (483 years x 365 days) & 173,880 days (383 years x 360 days) = 2415.

If you divide that by 366 days (leap years) you get 6.59 year

subtracted from 38 A.D., your
arrive at 32 A.D.

Should one attempt to present the
message of the Lord to the Jewish
people before these corner pieces have
been restored to the puzzle, his efforts
would be of little avail. He must be
shown that the teaching of the Old
Testament is in perfect accord with the
New; but, in order to do this, he must
first be given the correct interpretation
of the Old Testament predictions
relative to Messiah. One should never
mention anything about the New
Testament revelation until he has first
shown the Jewish truth-seeker what
are the teachings of his own Sacred
Writings. When this is done the
teaching of the New Testament can
easily be presented. It will be apparent
to anyone that its teachings are in

perfect alignment with those of Moses and the prophets.

CHAPTER 3

Restoring The Borders

The borders of the puzzle represent the framework of the entire puzzle.

The framework is the support system for the structural basis of the project.

It is the foundation or base from which the remainder of the puzzle can be completed.

One of the biggest stumbling blocks for the Jewish mindset, is that this border, this framework, this foundation, in his mind, was not constructed by a Jewish contractor, but by a bunch of antisemitic Gentile zealots attempting to start a new religion. That's what we were told our entire lives!

It's "Bubbe Meises"- Yiddish for "a grandmother's fables", or "old wives tales"…that's all we heard.

My nickname amongst friends is "The Ancient Of Days". For those of you who also "have one foot in the grave, and the other on a banana peel", you might remember the TV series of the 1950's "Dragnet". It was a "cops & robbers" drama that always began by telling the television audience that "the names have been changed, to protect the innocent".

Well, the names have been changed, but in my opinion, to deceive and confuse the innocent.

In Matthew 1:20-21 it reads: *an angel of the Lord appeared unto him in a dream, saying, Joseph, thou son of David, fear not to take unto thee Miriam thy wife: for that which is conceived in her is of the Holy Spirit.   And she shall bring forth a son; and thou shalt call his name YESHUA; for it is he that shall save his people from their sins.*

An Angel of the Lord told Joseph that the child's name shall be Yeshua(salvation in hebrew). It was a relatively popular name for a Jewish boy in the first century, easy to pronounce, and the shortened version of Joshua, Yehoshua.

Remarkably, almost every country has decided to change his name, despite what the Angel of the Lord told Joseph.

Here are just a few:

Iēsous Christós,Eashoa M'sheekha-Yasu' Al Masih Esa Al Masih- ,Jezu Krishti,Íosa Hisus K'ristos,Isus Krist-Yesu Khristu,Yēsū Jīdū ,Jezus Christus ,Jeesuse Kristuse- Hesu Kristo,Xesu Crist- Ieso Qriste, Yīśu Masīha- Yexus Khetos- Gesù Cristo-Ihu Karaiti- Jesoa Kristy- Hesu Kristu- Isus Hristos Iisus Khristos-

Ciise Masiix- Jesu Cristo - Isoi Maseh-
Iesu Grist- Jesu Kristu- Yesus Kristus.

I'm sorry, but none of those guys
sound Jewish to me!

Here are the names of famous people
most you would recognize.

Pablo Picasso, Pancho Villa, Roberto
Clemente, Fernando Lamas, Juan
Carlos, Leonardo DiVinci, Georgio
Armani, Silvio Berlusconi, Gianni
Versace, Cristiano Ronaldo, Pele
Santos, Vladimir Putin.

I could add hundreds to these twelve
names, and the conclusion would be
the same. These people would be
known by their given first names,
wherever and whenever they would
travel, from the time of their birth, to
even after their death. Pablo doesn't
become Paul, Juan doesn't become
John, and Leonardo does not become
Leonard.

Here's my point. We are trying to establish a Jewish foundation, a Jewish framework so we can continue to move forward. Remember, we are trying to help the Jewish person solve that portion of the puzzle. You would be amazed to find out how many people who claim to be Christians, don't even know that 'Jesus Christ" is a Jew!

American and Israeli Jews don't know his given name is Yeshua, because they have never heard him called anything other than "Jesus". The only Jesus we knew growing up was Jesus Alou, who played for the much hated San Francisco Giants baseball team, and he always made the sign of a cross in the dirt at home plate before he came up to bat!

In today's world of cyber technology, identity theft is a big issue. This is a form of identity theft that has far reaching consequences. Eternal consequences.

On a personal level, the first time I heard the name Yeshua was in a Messianic congregation. I kind of knew who the pastor was referring to, but something was different. Something supernatural was occurring, is the only way I could describe it. This was not the "Jesus" I had heard about my whole life. This was a different person that I wanted to know more about, is about the only way I can explain it. My testimony is not unique. Many Jewish people I know have shared the same story.

God uses Yeshua's given Jewish name to draw his people closer. It might be just a small piece of the puzzle, but it gives us the ability to move forward and to go find the next puzzle piece.

John the Baptist is another interesting character. You might think it funny, but most Jewish people believe John is a Baptist. Why wouldn't they, for crying out loud?

Remember, they haven't read any of the New Testament.

If you grew up in a predominantly Jewish neighborhood, there were no Jewish people named John who were Jewish. It just didn't happen. If your name was John, you were a Gentile. Yochanan is his Hebrew name, and The Immerser, rather than the Baptist will get you one step forward, rather than two steps backwards.

Mary of course was a Catholic ! At least that's what we were told. After all, she looked like a Catholic Nun in all of the pictures you see of her. And just like the name John, there were no Jewish girls with the name Mary. If your name was Mary, you were a Gentile. Always thought it odd that Moses's sister was Miriam, but Yeshua's mother was Mary!

Don't want to leave out The Apostle Paul. I must admit, I did know a Paul growing up that was Jewish- One. Now

Saul...that's a different story. I had several friends named Saul. But what is an Apostle anyway? We didn't know, and we didn't want to know. If his name was the Apostle Paul, he couldn't be Jewish.

Words and names are critical in what they connotate. They conjure up images in our mind. If I were to picture Jesus, John the Baptist, the Virgin Mary, and the Apostle Paul, I see the four of them all wearing crosses on their way to church!

You see this depicted in art form everywhere. This is what Jewish people see and what they think.

But if I picture Yeshua, his mother Miriam, Yochanan the Immerser, and Rabbi Saul celebrating Sukkot(The Feast of Tabernacles-John 7:37)or Chanukah(The Feast of Dedication-John 10:22), or Shavuot(Pentecost-Acts 2:1) or The Last Supper depicted as Passover(Luke 22:15) instead of

Easter, it now becomes a Jewish story and much more palatable, and gives us the ability to move forward and find the next piece of the puzzle.

Rabbi Burt Yellin in his book "Messiah- A Rabbinical And Scriptural Viewpoint", describes it this way".

"By the time of the first Council of Nicea (325 CE), any "Jewishness" associated with a faith in Yeshua had been obscured. Proselytization by the Jews was forbidden, and the Sabbath was forbidden and replaced with Sunday worship. The Passover meal was forbidden and changed to Easter. Jews who had accepted Yeshua as the Messiah were further informed that they could no longer continue in their previous form of worship, and upon assimilation into the now Catholic Church, had to take vows renouncing their former Jewish ties. We find in subsequent generations, the church drifted further and further from its

Hebrew culture and roots and from the land of Israel from which it sprang. It is the transformation of Yeshua HaMashiach, the Jewish Messiah, to Yesou Christou-Jesus, the Gentile Christ, that has perpetuated the unremitting doctrine that one cannot exist as a Jew and believe in Yeshua as the Messiah."

As I mentioned earlier in this chapter, we were told that the New Testament was an anti-Semitic document. If that is repeated to you over and over, you believe it, and would make sense as to why we wouldn't want to read it. We were told that Church history is filled with long and deep anti-Semitic rhetoric and some horrific historical proof of many deplorable acts.

Following, is a written document which is pretty representative of how many Jewish people think and what they have uncovered regarding its content, as well as quotes from church fathers and sordid church history.

It's a long read, but you must understand what you are up against when attempting to share the "Good News", and a crucial puzzle piece that must be dealt with.

ANTI-SEMITISM IN THE NEW TESTAMENT

Shmuel Golding

In recent years, many books have been written on the subject of anti-Semitism. Most of those books blame the church for its hostile teachings which encouraged ignorant devotees to harass, and even to violently assault Jews in the name of Christ and his church. Many Christian writers have openly acknowledged this fact and have called upon the church to make amends.

Yet, apologize as they may, none of them attack the root cause of

Christian anti-Semitism, which in my opinion lies in the New Testament itself. One writer from the gentile camp, who dares admit to this in his book *"The Misery of Christianity,"* is a former pastor by the name of Joachim Kahl. A writer from the Jewish side, Jules Isaac wrote a book entitled *"Jesus et Israel,"* in which he maintained that anti-Semitism begins with the New Testament. Apart from two voices, very few have been bold enough to place the blame where it belongs.

Father Gregory Baum states that when he read Isaac's book it shattered him, and so he set about on a task to counter-refute such claims, yet in the introduction he has to admit that at face value certain passages of the New Testament do appear to be anti-Semitic, but says Father

Baum all such verses can be explained.

Maybe they can be explained, the scriptures can be stretched this way and that way to make them say almost anything, but my bone of contention is that whilst those statements remain in print in the form of a holy book, men will use them to feed their hatred and the Jew will continue to suffer. Let history itself be our witness, and let history be the judge as to whether or not the roots of Christian anti-Semitism lie within the New Testament.

It will not be hard to prove that the roots of anti-Semitism lie in the New Testament and that its fruits have been plucked and digested by Christians from the earliest times until the present day.

Bible-intoxicated Christians through the ages have thrown in the teeth of the Jews the demonic charges of "Christ-killers" and have fanned the flames of Jew-hatred using the New Testament for their justification.

There are numerous verses found in the New Testament which have caused the blood of countless Jews to be shed throughout history. We will examine these verses and compare them with words said, and deeds committed against Jews by the church and its leaders.

These anti-Semitic statements were and still are the principal cause of all persecutions, oppressions and pogroms in which Jews have suffered. These anti-Semitic accounts in the New Testament have taught mankind to hate the Jew. As long as the New

Testament continues in print (at least in its present form) the Jew will be hated. Here are but a few verses from where Christianity borrowed its anti-Semitic sentiments.

"The children of the kingdom shall be cast out into outer darkness: there shall be weeping and gnashing of teeth." (Matthew 8.12)

"O Jerusalem, Jerusalem, thou that killest the prophets and stonest them that are sent unto thee, how often would I have gathered thy children together even as a hen gathereth her chickens under her wings, and ye would not! Behold your house is left unto you desolate." (Matthew 23.37,38) Then answered all the people (Jews) and said, "His blood be on us and on our children" (Matthew 27:25). [1] "But take heed to yourselves: for they shall deliver you to councils, and in the synagogues ye shall be beaten" (Mark 13.9)

"He that believeth not shall be damned" (Mark 16.16)

"Ye are of your father the devil and the lusts of your father ye will do. He was a murderer from the beginning, and abode not in the truth, because there is no truth in him. When he speaks a lie, he speaketh of his own: for he is a liar and the father of it. And because I tell you the truth, ye believe me not. Which of you convinceth me of sin? And I say the truth, why do you not believe me? He that is of God heareth God's words: ye therefore hear them not, because ye are not of God" (John 8.43-47)

"Stiff-necked and uncircumcised in heart and ears, ye do always resist the Holy Ghost: as your fathers did, so you do. Which of the prophets have not your fathers persecuted? and they have slain them which showed before of the coming of the Just One; of whom ye have been now the betrayers and murderers" (Acts 7.51-53)

"It was necessary that the word of God should first have been spoken to you: but seeing you put it from you and judge yourself unworthy of everlasting life, we turn to the Gentiles" (Acts 13.45-51)

"For there are many unruly and vain talkers and deceivers, specially they of the circumcision: whose mouths must be stopped, who subvert whole houses, teaching things which they ought not, for filthy lucre's sake ... wherefore rebuke them sharply, that they may be sound in the faith; not giving heed to Jewish fables and commandments of men, that turn from the truth." (Titus 1.10-14).

"The Jews, who both killed the Lord Jesus and their own prophets, and have persecuted us; and they please not God and are contrary to all men: forbidding us to speak to the Gentiles that they

might be saved, to fill up
their sins always: for the
wrath is come upon them
to the uttermost." (l
Thessalonians 2.14-16)

"Who is a liar but he that
denieth that Jesus is the
Christ? He is an
antichrist, that denieth the
father and the son.
Whoever denieth the son,
the same hath not the
father" (l John 2.22,23)

"I know the blasphemy of
them which say they are
Jews and are not, but are
the synagogue of Satan ..."
(Revelation 2.9,10)

"Behold I will make them of
the synagogue of Satan,
which say they are Jews
and are not but do lie;
behold I will make them to

come and worship before
thy feet..." (Revelation 3.9)

These vicious and treacherous
New Testament verses, have
given the impression that the
Jews in the time of Jesus were
degenerate and cruel and that
they are a deicide race. They
have been spread by the church
for the last two millennia, and
have not been rooted out of
Christian thinking to the present
day. Even those fundamentalist
lovers of Israel, only love the
Jews in order to save them from
the punishment awaiting them
for not having accepted Jesus.
They, as much, if not more than
any other Christian today,
believe that the Jew is guilty of
deicide and that his Judaism is
an old worn out rag which they
wish to replace with their New
Testament.

Moses Bazes, author of "*Jesus the Jew, the Historical Jesus,*" after examining the anti-Semitic statements in the New Testament writes:

"I believe that because of the anti-Jewish narratives of the New Testament, the Jews were hounded from one country to another, denied to live as human beings, denied to work as other people worked, denied to play as others played, were in no country at peace, in no era at peace and finally persecuted and massacred. This was all because of the Christian bigotry and hatred in the name of Jesus. Obviously it cannot be possible to regard Jesus as none other than the scourge of God for the Jews. The tragic existence of the Jews during 1900

years in the Diaspora, the hatred they experienced, the pogroms, persecutions, murders and the destructions they suffered, must be mainly attributed to anti- Jewish statements in the New Testament. Christianity introduced contempt for the Jew and is thus responsible for what happened in the Second World War at the Dachau Concentration camp in Germany and at the Auschwitz concentration camp in Poland. What was started at the Church Council at Nicea in 325 CE was duly completed in the concentration camps and crematories of Christian Germany where six million Jews perished."

We will now examine the words of some Christian "saints" and leaders and notice how their anti-Jewish expressions are based on New Testament verses listed earlier in this article.

Origen: "Their rejection of Jesus has resulted in their present calamity and exile. We say with confidence that they will never be restored to their former condition. For they have committed a crime of the most unhallowed kind, in conspiring against the saviour."

St. Gregory: " Jews are slayers of the Lord, murderers of the prophets, enemies of God, haters of God, adversaries of grace, enemies of their fathers' faith, advocates of the devil, brood of vipers, slanderers, scoffers, men of darkened minds, leaven of the Pharisees, congregation of demons, sinners, wicked men, stoners and haters of goodness."

St. Jerome: "....serpents, haters of all men, their image is Judas ... their psalms and prayers are the braying of donkeys.."

St. John Chrysostom: "I know that many people hold a high regard for the Jews and consider their way of life worthy of respect at the present time... This is why I am hurrying to pull up this fatal notion by the roots ... A place where a whore stands on display is a whorehouse. What is more, the synagogue is not only a whorehouse and a theater; it is also a den of thieves and a haunt of wild animals ... not the cave of a wild animal merely, but of an unclean wild animal ... When animals are unfit for work, they are marked for slaughter, and this is the very thing which the Jews have experienced. By making themselves unfit for work, they have become ready for slaughter. This is why Christ

said: "ask for my enemies, who
did not want me to reign over
them, bring them and slay them
before me' (Luke 19.27)."

St. Augustine: "Judaism is a
corruption. Indeed Judas is the
image of the Jewish people.
Their understanding of the
Scriptures is carnal. They bear
the guilt for the death of the
saviour, for through their
fathers they have killed the
Christ."

St. Thomas Aquinas: "It would be
licit to hold Jews, because of the
crimes, in perpetual servitude,
and therefore the princes may
regard the possessions of Jews as
belonging to the State."

The teachings of Martin Luther:

"Know, 0 adored Christ, and
make no mistake, that
aside from the Devil, you

have no enemy more
venomous, more
desperate, more bitter,
than a true Jew who truly
seeks to be a Jew... a Jew,
a Jewish heart, are hard as
wood, as stone, as iron, as
the Devil himself. In
short, they are children of
the Devil, condemned to
the flames of hell."

"O Lord, I am too feeble to
mock such devils. I would
do so, but they are much
stronger than I in raillery,
and they have a God who
is a past master in this art;
He is called the devil and
the wicked spirit.. They
have transformed God
into the devil, or rather
into a servant of the Devil,
accomplishing all the evil
the Devil desires,
corrupting unhappy souls ,
and raging against

himself: in short, the Jews are worse than the devils."

"What then shall we Christians do with this damned, rejected race of Jews? First, their synagogues should be set on fire, and whatever does not burn up should be covered or spread over with dirt so that no one may ever be able to see a cinder or stone of it. And this ought to be done for the honour of God and of Christianity, in order that God may see that we are true Christians. Secondly, their homes should be likewise broken down and destroyed. Thirdly, they should be deprived of their prayer books and Talmud's in which such idolatry, lies, cursing and blasphemy are taught.

Fourthly, their rabbis must be forbidden under threats of death to teach anymore."

"Now whoever wishes to accept venomous serpents, desperate enemies of the lord, and to honor them, to let himself be robbed, pillaged, corrupted and cursed by them, need only turn to the Jews. If this is not enough for him, he can do more: crawl up into their...... and worship the sanctuary, so as to glorify himself afterwards for having been merciful, for having fortified the Devil and his children, in order to blaspheme our beloved lord and the precious blood that has redeemed us. He will then be a perfect Christian, filled with works of mercy, for which Christ will reward him on the-day of judgment with the eternal fire of hell (where he will roast together with the Jews)."

"In truth, the Jews, being foreigners, should possess nothing, and what they do possess should be ours."

"...Cursed goy that I am, I cannot understand how they manage to be so skillful, unless I think that when Judas Iscariot hanged himself, his guts burst and emptied. Perhaps the Jews sent their servants with plates of silver and pots of gold to gather up Judas' piss with the other treasures, and then they ate and drank his offal, and thereby acquired eyes so piercing that they discover in the scriptures commentaries that neither Matthew nor Isaiah himself found there, not to mention the rest of us cursed goyim.."

"If I find a Jew to baptize, I shall lead him to the Elbe bridge, hang a stone around his neck, and push him into the water, baptizing him with the name of Avraham!.. I cannot convert the Jews. Our lord Christ did not succeed in doing so; but I can close their mouths so that there will be nothing for them to do but to lie upon the ground."

"I hope I shall never be so stupid as to be circumcised; I would rather cut off the left

breast of my Catherine
and of all women."

"If we are to remain unsullied
by the blasphemy of the
Jews and not wish to take
part in it, we must be
separated from them and
they must be driven out of
their country."

These anti-semitic words
uttered by popes, priests,
pastors and laymen, were
put into action by unruly
Christian mobs and later
by Hitler's followers.

Adolf Hitler: "I believe that I am
today acting according to the
purposes of the Almighty
Creator. In resisting the Jew, I
am fighting the Lord's battle."

Now let us apply these sayings to
deeds committed by Christians

who took their New Testament literally.

The crusader's sword found its justification in the words of Matthew 10.34, *"I have not come to bring peace on earth but a sword."* The Inquisitor's fire found its justification in the words of John 15.6, *"If a man abide not in me, he is cast forth as a branch, and is withered; and men gather them, and cast them into the fire and they are burned."* The cancellation of debts owed to Jews, found its justification in the parable recorded in Luke 16. The first blood libel was made by Jesus himself where in Matthew 23.35, he states *"that upon you may come all the righteous blood shed upon the earth, from the blood of righteous Abel unto the blood of Zacharias son of Barachias, whom ye slew between the temple and the altar."*

Rev William Hull

At the time of the World
Pentecostal Conference in
Jerusalem in 1961, Hull, a
Canadian Missionary, wrote two
articles entitled *"Christian
Analysis of Current Events in
Israel"* for Christian News from
Israel (published by the Ministry
of Religious Affairs). In these he
analyzed political, cultural and
social developments in the
country in the light of his unique
method of interpretations. He
also discussed the significance of
the Eichmann Trial, [2] which was
then being held in Jerusalem.
That subject had special interest
for him, since at his request he
had been appointed by the
authorities as Eichmann's
confessor.

Hull visited Eichmann in his cell 14
times, and tried to convert him
to a belief in Jesus as the savior,
so that he might atone for his

actions. However, Hull's efforts proved fruitless. Later he wrote a book describing those conversations with Eichmann, but the content of the talks and certain statements made by Hull subsequent to those talks, evoked a negative reaction in various Jewish circles. Criticism was directed mainly at the extreme Fundamentalist position, in accordance with which Hull had promised Eichmann that God would forgive his sins if in a written statement he would declare his acceptance of Christ. In Canada, Hull told the correspondent of a Toronto newspaper that the six million Jewish victims of the Nazis were doomed to perish in hell, and would not enter paradise, because they had not accepted the belief in Christ. Moreover, he said, Eichmann's sins were not as great as those of the average man who denied Jesus as the redeemer. (From *"American Fundamentalism and Israel"* by Yona Malachy)

German Christians under Hitler Paul Althaus, a Lutheran theologian of renown in Germany, warmly greeted the rise of Hitler. He wrote that, "The Protestant churches have greeted the political turning point as a gift and miracle of God".. *("Die deutsche Stunde der Kirche,"* p.5)

Many times Althaus explained to Christians his preference for the Third Reich over the former Weimar Republic. "We Christians know," he stated, "that we are bound by God's will to the promotion of National Socialism, so that all members of the people will be ready for service and sacrifice." (*"Kirche and Staat,"* p. 29)

In a document signed by many Christian theologians it was stated, "We as believing Christians thank God our Father that he has given to our people in its time of need the Fuhrer as a pious and faithful sovereign, and that he wants to prepare for us in the National Socialist system of government, good rule, a government with discipline and honor. Accordingly, we know that we are responsible before God to assist the work of the Fuhrer in our calling and in our station in life.". (*"Ansbacher Ratschlag,"* p. 145)

Another high ranking Christian theologian, Leutheuser, believed that the Holy Spirit moves where it chooses, and stated that, "more spirit of religion has come to Germans through Hitler, than through many of the churches." (Julius Leutheuser. *"Die deutsche Christusgemeinde,"* p. 18,19) This same Christian leader asserts that "Germany has been given a mission from God. The leader and prophet is Adolf Hitler." (SiegfriedLeffer. *"Christus im Drittem Reich der Deutschen,"* p. 13-18)

The Vatican under Pope Pius XII made a Concordat of collaboration with National Socialism. Hitler's portrait was placed on all walls of Catholic churches and Sunday schools. Church bells were rang at every Nazi victory, including the arrest and transportation of the last Jew from every town in Germany. The Roman Catholic Church never protested against Hitler's barbarism including the massacre of a million and a half Jewish children.. (*Dictionary of Antisemitism*, p. 43)

At a Church conference, Hitler
affirmed that the Catholic
Church has always regarded
Jews as evildoers and had
banished them into ghettos. He
(Hitler) is only doing what the
Church had been doing for
fifteen hundred years.. (ibid, p.
79)

In fact the Catholic youth
organisation of Germany was
combined with the Hitler youth
following the signing of the
Concordat of Collaboration
sponsored by Msgr. Pacelli later
to become Pope Pius XII.
Together they sang the
Horstwessel Lied in the church
vestries "Wenn das Judenblut
vom Messer spritzed".. ('When
Jewish blood runs off the
dagger,' ibid, p. 109)

In a speech to Polish Catholics,
Hitler declared: "I as a German
Catholic, ask only what is

permitted to Polish Catholics. To be antisemitic is not to be un-Catholic. The Church used every weapon against the Jews, even the Inquisition. Christ himself was a pioneer in the fight against Judaism." (ibid, p. 146)

An interesting quotation appears in the *Encyclopedia Britannica* under "German Christians:"

"Protestants who attempted to subordinate church policy to the political exigencies of Nazi Germany. The German Christians' Faith Movement, organized in 1932, was nationalistic and so anti-Semitic that extremists wished to repudiate the Old Testament and the Pauline Letters because of their Jewish authorship. In July 1933 the state territorial churches merged to form

the German Evangelical
Church, and in September
the German Christian
candidate, Ludwig Muller,
became Reichsbishop.
Muller's efforts to make
the church an instrument
of Nazi policy were
resisted by the Confessing
Church, under the
leadership of Martin
Niemoller. After World
War II the German
Christian Church party
was banned."

Are present day Christian attitudes
towards the Jews any better?
Liberals say they are, and they
continue to call for tolerance and
understanding. But the
fundamentalists are hindering
and harming the progress that
has been made in Christian-
Jewish relationships. By their
desire to convert the Jew, they
prove themselves to be the most

anti-Semitic of all Christian groups, for the whole idea of conversion is anti-Semitic.

Christian missionary love for the Jew is a kind of hatred. It loves the Jew, yet hates him for being what he is. It sees him as blind and in need of being changed into a believer. When missionary efforts failed, or are foiled, the love for the Jew quickly turns to hatred and contempt.

We are not deceived by the 'new Christians' of today's hand-clapping fundamentalists. They teach the same anti-Semitic doctrines as the church of yesteryear. Their tactics are different but we know that the message is the same. Any Jew who can pay homage to the New Testament or allow himself to believe in it, is, in my opinion in the same category as a Jew who

tries to justify Hitler's Mein
Kampf or, as one who covers up
for the deeds of the Nazis.

More Jews have been affected, hurt
or killed, in the name of Christ
and his church during the last
two thousand years than those
massacred by the Nazis. Yet
there are Jews, who being so
alienated from their own people,
have overlooked this fact and
have joined themselves to the
church with its built-in anti-
Semitism.

To imagine that this Jewish self
curse and curse on their children
(Matthew 27:25) was actually
uttered by any group of Jews is a
violation of respect for the
human intellect and a travesty.
Because of the depth and spread
of this Christian belief – and the
evil it has wrought – it is most
necessary to refute and discredit

Matthew 27:25 beyond any shadow of doubt.

The Jewish child is the 'hero' of the Brith Milah (Circumcision): the Bar-Mitzvah and nowadays the Bat-Mitzvah (Confirmation of male and female children as Subjects of the Commandment); the Passover Seder (Feast of Mazot); and the Pidyon ha'Ben (Redemption of the First-born son)...

There is scarcely a single religious rite of the Jew that is complete without the participation of the child. An entire chapter of the Holy Scriptures, "Proverbs," is devoted to the proper upbringing of the Jewish child - its first seven chapters are addressed to "My Son". Even after the Jew's passing from his life the connection between parent and child is perpetuated through the son's recital of the

Kaddish prayer in memory of the departed parent. Thus, from birth to after death in a never-ending cycle, the Jew and his child are inseparable. It has always been so since Judaism began and it will always be so...

As for the "Blood curse" (Matthew 27:25), oceans of ink have been expended by bible scholars Christian and Jewish - starting two centuries ago, to demonstrate that this self-curse and curse on the children of Israel could never have been uttered. Despite this, rivers of Jewish blood have been spilled by a blind and unbending fanaticism that persisted, and still persists, in perpetuating the fiction that the self-curse was actually voiced. Since the Catholic Church and fundamentalist Protestant sects consider every word in the New Testament to be the "Word of

God," Matthew 27:25 is a dogma of the church.

They care because they know that Adolf Hitler's mendacious claim: "I believe that I am today acting in accordance with the will of the Almighty Creator; by defending myself against the Jew, I am fighting for the work of the Lord…" has Matthew 27:25 at its base. (A. Hitler, *MEIN KAMPF*, pg. 65; cf. E.H. Flannery, op. cit. pg. 2 1 0).

Harenberg continues: "It was Rudolf Bultmann who stated in 1921, with the help of the form critical method which he had developed, that this curse was never spoken" (c.f R. Bultrnann, *History of the Synoptic Tradition*, Harper, 1963, pg. 282).

The French historian Charles Guignebert wrote in 1935 about Matthew 27:25 directly, and of other passages of the same ilk in the New Testament, as follows: *"Few of the sayings of the Gospels have done more harm than these, and yet they are only the invention of a redactor"*. (C. Guignebert, *Jesus*, op. cit., pg. 470) Hitler used Jesus' name quite glibly to justify his unspeakable crimes.

It was the evangelist Matthew, not a redactor, who "invented" verse 27:25, but no matter, the damage is the same regardless of who the 'inventor' really was. The pity of it is that all anti-Semitic monsters use (and have used) the "poison" that is found in Christianity's Holy Book as propaganda to further their nefarious ends. Hitler was but one of many.

A million of the Jewish victims of the Holocaust were children.

Wow, it can and will be challenging
if faced with questions regarding
the Holocaust, The Inquisition,
The Crusades, as well as the
writings of some of the church
fathers listed above. Regarding
the New Testament scriptures
referred to by the author, the
Word of God stands on its own.
It is more of an indictment on
these well known church fathers
use of those scriptures, or should
I say misuse, and the damaging
affect it has had in Judeo-
Christian relations.

On a personal level, the very first
time I began reading the New
Testament I had two
overwhelming realizations. First,
I knew I was reading truth, and
second, this was not anti-Semitic
at all. The story we had been

told our whole lives just was not
accurate.

The pages of the New Testament

clearly follow the framework of
Judaism. The first four books,

the gospels, addressed a Jewish
audience. They echoed the
pattern of historical narratives
interspersed with instruction
found in the Torah. The
controversies between Yeshua
and the Scribes/Pharisees have
no reference outside the
community of Israel; Yeshua's
preaching of the coming
kingdom could have had
meaning only for Jews; the
synagogues in which Yeshua
reads from the prophets, heals
the sick, and forgives sins are
Jewish houses of worship for
believing Jews and not

unconverted gentiles. The Jewish festivals that are celebrated throughout the pages of the New Testament were not feasts of interest to the gentiles but were part of the daily life of the Jewish people.

A Jewish man named Avi Lipkin, an Israeli who ran for Prime Minister in the most recent elections held,(April 2019) insists that the New Testament is not anti-Semitic. "Jewish people ought to read the New Testament," he said. "I tell all my Jewish friends they ought to read the New Testament; and their response to me is, 'What are you? A "Jew for Jesus?"' I answer no, but if you read the New Testament for yourself, you will find out what Christians really believe. They respond by saying, 'Why should we read the New Testament? We don't even read the Old Testament.'"

It is important to understand that regardless of which testament is read, the reading must be done using the golden rule of interpretation:

When the plain sense of Scripture makes common sense, seek no other sense; therefore, take every word at its primary, ordinary, usual, literal meaning unless the facts of the immediate context studied in the light of related passages and axiomatic and fundamental truths, indicate clearly otherwise.

In Eitan Bar's new book, "Refuting Rabbinic Objections To Christianity & Messianic Prophesies" he writes:

"Here are the words of the Apostle Paul in the New Testament:

"I ask, then, has God rejected his people? By no means! For I myself am an Israelite, a descendant of Abraham, a member of the tribe of Benjamin. God has not rejected his people whom he foreknew." (Romans 11:1-2) And in another place Paul writes: *"I am*

*speaking the truth in Christ—I am not
lying; my conscience bears me witness
in the Holy Spirit- that I have great
sorrow and unceasing anguish in my
heart. For I could wish that I myself
were accursed and cut off from Christ
for the sake of my brothers, my kinsmen
according to the flesh. They are
Israelites, and to them belong the
adoption, the glory, the covenants, the
giving of the law, the worship, and the
promises. To them belong the
patriarchs, and from their race,
according to the flesh, is the Christ, who
is God over all, blessed forever."*
(Romans 9:1-5)

Those who decide to check for
themselves will find that Yeshua and
the New Testament are not anti-
Semitic at all. On the contrary, Yeshua
and his Apostles were not only Jewish,
but *loved* the people whom they
themselves belonged to. They loved
them so much that they could not
stand back and keep quiet any longer

in face of all the religious hypocrisy and corruption that was oppressing their people."

Paul tells us in the Book of Acts 17:11 *These were more noble than those in Thessalonica, in that they received the word with all readiness of mind, and <u>searched the scriptures daily, whether those things were so.</u>*
Where are the Berean's when you need them?

We have restored the corners of the puzzle in Chapter Two, and have now restored the borders, the framework of the puzzle here in this chapter, by showing that this is a Jewish story about Jewish people, and the New Testament is not an anti-Semitic piece of literature, but books written almost exclusively by Jewish men(which Jewish people are unaware of), including eye

witness accounts of those who
were in his select circle.

We can now continue to build the
puzzle slowly, with the many
remaining pieces that are left.

CHAPTER FOUR

"Bits & Pieces"

Following, are random puzzle
  pieces, that will assist the
  truth seeker into bringing
  the picture into clearer
  focus.

Micah 4:8 As for you, O watchtower
  of the flock, O stronghold of the
  Daughter of Zion, the former
  dominion will be restored to you;
  kingship will come to the Daughter
  of Jerusalem."

There are many who are not aware of
  the very deep significance of
  Bethlehem, Yeshua's (Jesus')
  birthplace. Everyone knows that
  Bethlehem was a place where
  shepherds grazed their sheep, and
  where the Messiah was to be born
  (Micah 5:2), but do not realize that
  it was a town designated as the

birthing place for lambs which were used for the Passover sacrifice. The Scriptures give significant details about this little town lying slightly south of Jerusalem.

In Micah 4:8 we read about the _"watchtower of the flock"_, or in Hebrew, "Migdal Edar." According to the "Life and Times of Jesus the Messiah", by Alfred Edersheim, a Jewish believer in the late 1800's, Migdal Edar was the location where the Messiah was to be revealed. This watchtower stood as a place of protection for the city from approaching enemies, but it was also utilized by shepherds to watch over the specific flocks from which sacrificial Passover lambs were taken.

The shepherds who were tending

these particular flocks were no ordinary shepherds. They were specifically trained by the Rabbis for a holy task. They had to insure that, as much as possible, every lamb was free of any blemish or injury, in order to be used for the Passover sacrifice. Since they were instructed by the Rabbis, they almost certainly knew of those passages in the Targum's (Aramaic translations) and the Mishna associating the birth of the Messiah with "Migdal Edar". For example, Migdal Edar is translated in one of the Targums as *"The Anointed One of the Flock of Israel."* It is also written in the Mishna that "He spread his tent beyond Migdal Edar, the place where King Messiah will reveal Himself at the end of days."

If you were to Google the name Yinnon-You would find it is one of names of Messiah.

After reading Psalm 72, the Rabbi's understood the text to be speaking about the Messiah. In verse 17 it reads;   His name shall endure forever: his name shall be <u>continued</u> as long as the sun: and *men* shall be blessed in him: all nations shall call him blessed.

The word "continued" is the word "yinnon", which means perpetual. The text continues and says "as long as the sun".In the Hebrew it actually says "*<u>before</u>* the sun his name was Yinnon"; as does the Targum (Aramaic translation of the Old Testament), "<u>before the sun was</u>, or was created, his name was prepared;" or appointed: for they say the name of the Messiah was one of the seven things created before the world was: it is certain that Messiah was the Son of God, from eternity, or the eternal Son of God: he was so before his resurrection from the dead, when he was only declared, and did not then become the Son of God: he was owned by his divine Father, and believed in as the Son of God by men before that time: he was so before his incarnation, and not by that: he, the Son of God, was sent in human nature, and made manifest in it, and was known by David and Solomon, under that relation; and, as such, he was concerned in the creation of all things; and was in the day of eternity, and from all eternity, the only begotten Son of the Father."

We have listed many prophesies from the Old Testament that we believe were fulfilled in the life, death, and resurrection of Yeshua. To prove the validity of the Old Testament, here are some facts that you probably weren't aware of!

ADVANCED MEDICAL KNOWLEDGE IN THE HEBREW BIBLE

Medical science did not know of the existence of germs and their methods of transmission of infection until the end of the last century!

People had no idea that invisible & deadly microscopic germs could exist on eating and cooking utensils

Leviticus 6:28, written of 3500 years ago, give clear commandments to discard broken pottery & metal pots

should be disinfected by scouring &
rinsing in water.

Moses writings reveal an astonishing
knowledge of deadly germs associated
with dead animal bodies & anything
they touch. Leviticus 11:35 deals with
this.

Leviticus 7:24 forbids the people to eat
the flesh of any animal that has died
naturally of disease or by wild animals.

Numbers 19:14-17 deals with
advanced sanitation laws to prevent
the spread of infection. Throughout
human history mankind has suffered
billions of untold deaths due to
infection & microscopic germs. Germs
from a dead human body are more

dangerous to another human than germs from an animal's body because of greater likelihood of transmission of disease

Throughout history the scourge of leprosy has killed untold millions of people and afflicted many more with misery

Amazingly, an examination of the detailed laws of Numbers & Leviticus reveal an advanced system for the control of infectious diseases at a time when ancient pagan nations did not understand the dangers of infections. <u>Leviticus 13:43-46</u>

Over 60 Million people , almost 1/3 of the population of Europe in the 14th

Century are estimated to have died by
the Black Death-Bubonic Plague.

The history at that time reveals that
the doctors could do nothing. It was
only after the people began to follow
the ancient biblical laws of sanitation
and disease control that the epidemic
was broken

Church leaders in Vienna began to
search the bible to discover whether or
not there was a practical biblical
solution.

They discovered in Leviticus 13:46
that Moses laid down strict regulations
from God regarding the medical
treatment of those afflicted with
Leprosy or Plague

The divine medical rule demanded that a person who contracted leprosy or the plague must be isolated and segregated from the general population during his infectious period, until he was healed or died-QUARANTINE

God's basic sanitation order regarding human waste for children of Israel was recorded in Deuteronomy 23:12,13 (read in different translation)

Military history notes that the vast majority of soldiers who have been killed during the countless wars have succumbed to infectious disease rather than bullets or other weapons of war.

Sickness & Plague often determined the outcome of a battle.

Prior to 1900, 5 times as many soldiers from disease that from anything else!

Statements Consistent With Biology

- The book of Leviticus (written prior to 1400 BC) describes the value of blood.

        <u>Leviticus 17:11</u>
        'For the life of the flesh *is* in the blood, and I have given it to you upon the altar to make atonement for your souls; for it *is* the blood *that* makes atonement for the soul.'

    The blood carries water and nourishment to every cell, maintains the body's temperature, and removes the waste material of the body's

cells. The blood also carries
oxygen from the lungs
throughout the body. In 1616,
William Harvey discovered that
blood circulation is the key
factor in physical life—
confirming what the Bible
revealed 3,000 years earlier.

- The Bible describes biogenesis
(the development of living
organisms from other living
organisms) and the stability of
each kind of living organism.

> <u>Genesis 1:11,12</u>
> Then God said, "Let the
> earth bring forth grass,
> the herb *that* yields seed,
> *and* the fruit tree *that*
> yields fruit according to its
> kind, whose seed *is* in
> itself, on the earth"; and it
> was so. And the earth
> brought forth grass, the

herb *that* yields seed
according to its kind, and
the tree *that* yields fruit,
whose seed *is* in itself
according to its kind. And
God saw that *it was* good.

Genesis 1:21
So God created great sea
creatures and every living
thing that moves, with
which the waters
abounded, according to
their kind, and every
winged bird according to
its kind. And God saw that
it was good.

Genesis 1:25
And God made the beast

of the earth according to its kind, cattle according to its kind, and everything that creeps on the earth according to its kind. And God saw that *it was* good.

The phrase "according to its kind" occurs repeatedly, stressing the reproductive integrity of each kind of animal and plant. Today we know this occurs because all of these reproductive systems are programmed by their genetic codes.

- The Bible describes the chemical nature of flesh.

<u>Genesis 2:7</u>
And the LORD God formed man *of* the dust of the ground, and breathed into his nostrils the breath

of life; and man became a
living being.

Genesis 3:19

By the sweat of your face You will
eat bread,

Till you return to the ground, Because
from it you were taken;

For you are dust, And to dust you
shall return."

- It is a proven fact that a person's
mental and spiritual health is
strongly correlated with physical
health. The Bible revealed this to
us with these statements (and
others) written by King Solomon
about 950 BC.

Proverbs 12:4

An excellent wife *is* the
crown of her husband,
But she who causes shame
is like rottenness in his
bones.

Proverbs 14:30

A sound heart *is* life to the
body,
But envy *is* rottenness to
the bones.

Proverbs 15:30

The light of the eyes
rejoices the heart,
And a good report makes
the bones healthy.

Proverbs 16:24
Pleasant words *are like* a
honeycomb,
Sweetness to the soul and
health to the bones.

Proverbs 17:22
A merry heart does good,
***like* medicine,**
But a broken spirit dries
the bones.

Eighth Day Circumcision

Doctors today know very well that it is best to perform circumcision on the eighth day of a child's life. On the eighth day there is more Vitamin K and prothrombin present in the blood, which means less pain, less bleeding, and a better healing process.

For those who struggle with the fact that Yeshua actually existed. This portion is for you.

HISTORICAL EVIDENCE FOR YESHUA OF NAZARETH

Flavius Josephus

Joseph ben Matthias was born in the year 37 C.E. and died around 100 C.E. As the son of a Jewish priest he eventually became a priest himself and member of the Pharisee sect of Judaism.

In 64 C.E. he went to Rome to secure the release of certain priests and became convinced that Rome could not be defeated by the Jewish revolt which began in 66 C.E. and ended in 70 C.E.

In July 67 C.E. he was captured by Rome and was eventually hired as a scribe and an interpreter by the Roman government. At that time he was given the name Flavius Josephus by his Roman associates and wrote under that name.

In 70 C.E. he rode into Jerusalem with the Roman General Titus and observed the annihilation of Jerusalem. Josephus recorded incredibly graphic details about the destruction of Jerusalem as well as the crucifixion and death of millions of Jews.

There are 3 passages in his writings that are pertinent to Yeshua. In his

Antiquities of the Jews, book 18, chapter 3 he makes a comment about Yeshua.

"Now there was about this time, Yeshua, a wise man, if it is to be lawful to call him a man, for he was a doer of wonderful works- a teacher of such men as received the truth with pleasure. He drew over to him both many of the Jews and many of the gentiles. He was the Messiah;(*"perhaps the Messiah" in the Arabic version*) and when Pilate, at the suggestion of the principal men amongst us, had condemned him to the cross, those that loved him at the first did not forsake him, for he appeared to them alive again the third day, as the divine prophets had foretold these and ten thousand other wonderful things concerning him; and the tribe of

Christians so named for him, are not extinct at this day."

This testimony, called the *Testimonium Flavianum*, is a very controversial passage.

Critics have claimed that it was a Christian insertion. However, there is strong evidence from the ancient manuscripts that this passage was in the original, and is quoted by early Church Father Eusebius, as early as 325 C.E.

Ancient Rabbinical Reverences toYeshua

As expected, references to Yeshua are very unflattering. However, they do verify a number of important historical facts that the Gospels proclaim regarding Yeshua of Nazareth

No one doubted that Yeshua was a historical figure until about 200-300 years ago. The myth theory was created and perpetrated by atheists and agnostics and embraced by mainstream Judaism during the Renaissance.

In the Babylonian Talmud, which was compiled between the years 200-500 C.E.; in Sanhedrin 43a, there a fascinating reference to Jesus of Nazareth:

"It has been taught: On the Eve of the Passover, they hanged Yeshua. And an announcer went out in front of him, for 40 days saying: 'he is going to be stoned because he practiced sorcery and enticed and led Israel astray. Anyone who knows anything in his favor, let him come and plead in his behalf.' But, not having found anything in his favor, they hanged him on the Eve of Passover.

It is interesting to note that the miracles were explained away as being from a demonic source. Also, it is illegal to perform capital punishment on the Eve of Passover, something we wouldn't expect to find verified in a Rabbinic source.

The writer has verified that Yeshua is indeed a historical figure!

Maimonides

Maimonides was a very highly revered 13th Century Rabbi. It has been said "there was never a greater man than Maimonides except Moses". He was given the nickname "Rambam"

He wrote a 14 volume work called the Mishna Torah in which he made multiple references to the historical existence of Yeshua. However in 1631, Catholic & Jewish authorities censored much of it, removing all references of Yeshua because of highly derogatory references.

During the Spanish Inquisition certain members of the Catholic Church used his works and negative references to justify the killing of Jews.

An excerpt from the uncensored versions of the Mishna Torah is a remarkable historical reference to Yeshua.

"Jesus of Nazareth, who aspired to be the Messiah and was executed by the court was also alluded to in Daniel's prophesies (11:14) as the "vulgar common among your people shall exalt themselves in an attempt to fulfill the vision, but they shall stumble. _Can there be a greater stumbling block than Christianity_ " (Isa.8:14)

Ultimately, all the deeds of Jesus of Nazareth and that Ishmaelite Mohammed who arose after him will only serve to prepare the way for Messiah's coming and the improvement of the entire world to serve God together, as Zephaniah 3:9 states.

Crucifixion was invented by the Persians in 300-400BC and developed, during Roman times, into a punishment for the most serious of criminals. The upright wooden cross was the most common technique, and the time victims took to die would depend on how they were crucified.

King David wrote the 22nd Psalm around 1,000BC

Most bible experts would agree, David was given a vision of Yeshua during his crucifixion.

Below is Psalm 22 in its entirety, as well as New Testament references depicting the crucifixion.

Psalm 22   [1] My God, my God, why have you forsaken me?

    Why are you so far from saving me,
    so far from my cries of anguish?
[2] My God, I cry out by day, but you do not answer,

    by night, but I find no rest.

[3] Yet you are enthroned as the Holy One;

    you are the one Israel praises.
[4] In you our ancestors put their trust;
    they trusted and you delivered them.
[5] To you they cried out and were saved;

    in you they trusted and were not put to shame.

⁶ But I am a worm and not a man,
  scorned by everyone, despised by
the people.
⁷ All who see me mock me;
  they hurl insults, shaking their
heads.
⁸ "He trusts in the LORD," they say,
  "let the LORD rescue him.
Let him deliver him,
  since he delights in him."

⁹ Yet you brought me out of the womb;
  you made me trust in you, even at
my mother's breast.
¹⁰ From birth I was cast on you;
  from my mother's womb you have
been my God.

¹¹ Do not be far from me,
  for trouble is near
  and there is no one to help.

¹² Many bulls surround me;
  strong bulls of Bashan encircle me.
¹³ Roaring lions that tear their prey
  open their mouths wide against me.
¹⁴ I am poured out like water,

and all my bones are out of joint.
My heart has turned to wax;
    it has melted within me.
¹⁵ My mouth is dried up like a
potsherd,
    and my tongue sticks to the roof of
my mouth;
    you lay me in the dust of death.

¹⁶ Dogs surround me,
    a pack of villains encircles me;
    they pierce my hands and my feet.
¹⁷ All my bones are on display;
    people stare and gloat over me.
¹⁸ They divide my clothes among them
    and cast lots for my garment.

¹⁹ But you, LORD, do not be far from
me.
    You are my strength; come quickly
to help me.
²⁰ Deliver me from the sword,
    my precious life from the power of
the dogs.
²¹ Rescue me from the mouth of the
lions;

   save me from the horns of the wild
oxen.

²² I will declare your name to my
people;
   in the assembly I will praise you.
²³ You who fear the LORD, praise him!
   All you descendants of Jacob, honor
him!
   Revere him, all you descendants of
Israel!
²⁴ For he has not despised or scorned
   the suffering of the afflicted one;
he has not hidden his face from him
   but has listened to his cry for help.

²⁵ From you comes the theme of my
praise in the great assembly;
   before those who fear you I will
fulfill my vows.
²⁶ The poor will eat and be satisfied;
   those who seek the LORD will praise
him—
   may your hearts live forever!

²⁷ All the ends of the earth
   will remember and turn to the

Lord,
and all the families of the nations
   will bow down before him,
²⁸ for dominion belongs to the Lord
   and he rules over the nations.

²⁹ All the rich of the earth will feast
and worship;
   all who go down to the dust will
kneel before him—
   those who cannot keep themselves
alive.
³⁰ Posterity will serve him;
   future generations will be told about
the Lord.
³¹ They will proclaim his righteousness,
   declaring to a people yet unborn:
   He has done it!

The New Testament makes numerous
allusions to Psalm 22, mainly during
the crucifixion of Jesus.

- **Psalm 22:1, "My God, my God,
  why have you forsaken me?"**, is

quoted in <u>Mark 15:34</u>; <u>Matthew 27:46</u>

- <u>Psalm 22:7</u>, "They hurl insults, shaking their heads", is quoted in <u>Mark 15:29</u>; <u>Matthew 27:39</u>
- <u>Psalm 22:8</u>, "He trusted on the Lord that he would deliver him: let him deliver him, seeing he delighted in him", is quoted in <u>Matthew 27:43</u>
- <u>Psalm 22:18</u>, "They divide my clothes among them and cast lots for my garment", is quoted in <u>Mark 15:24</u>; <u>Matthew 27:35</u>; <u>Luke 23:34</u>; <u>John 19:24</u>
- <u>Psalm 22:22</u>, "I will declare your name to my people; in the assembly I will praise you", is quoted <u>Hebrews 2:12</u>

I have titled this next puzzle piece:

One Messiah, Two Messiah's or No Messiah's

The following great article written by "Bibles For Israel" brings into focus a debate that has been raging for centuries.

"Christians often think that Jewish people reject the idea that Messiah would be resurrected. But it is an ancient belief that persists to this very day.

In the *Canadian Jewish News* on January 17, 2002, we read:

"Our long-awaited messiah and redeemer arrived! Most Jews failed to recognize that he was the messiah, but we, his disciples, did. Tragically, he died before completing the redemptive process. But he will soon be resurrected and will continue and complete his messianic tasks."

This newspaper article records the ideas and thoughts held by a Hassidic sect of Jewish people called Lubavitch, who believe that their Rebbe Menachem Mendel Schneerson was and is the Messiah.

Soon after his death, they launched a worldwide multimillion dollar campaign with full-page newspaper ads declaring their faith in his Messiahship. That campaign continues today on buses and billboards throughout Israel and Jewish communities worldwide.

Chabad-"Halachic Ruling" declaring "every single Jew" had to believe in the imminent second coming of the deceased 7th Lubavitcher Rebbe as the Messiah, signed by nearly 250 Lubavitch Rabbis.

This idea of a resurrected Messiah is not new.

As far back as AD 590–630, a Jewish apocalyptic book was written in the style of Ezekiel and Daniel called *Zerubbabel*. In it, Messiah ben Joseph

(called Nehemiah ben Hushiel in this book) dies in battle with the King of Edom (Armilus). However, Messiah Ben David arrives soon after and raises
him from the dead.

Rabbis believe that Messiah ben Joseph will fight in the great battle against Gog and Magog described in Ezekiel 38–39, and that he will die defending Israel against her enemies, only to be raised by Messiah ben David.

Why do ancient and modern Rabbis alike think that Messiah will be raised from the grave?

Rabbis have not made up the idea that Messiah will be raised from the dead.

They refer to Scriptures such as Psalm 16:10: "For You will not abandon my soul to Sheol; Nor will You allow Your Holy One to undergo decay."

As well, the Talmud says that when Messiah ben David sees Messiah ben Joseph slain, he will ask the Lord of the Universe for ben Joseph to receive "the gift of life."

The Lord then answers that "your father David has already prophesied this
concerning you" when David wrote, "He asked you for life, and you gave it to him—length of days, for ever and ever." *(Babylonian Talmud Sukkah 52a;*
Psalm 21:4, v. 5 in the Hebrew Bible)

While the Jewish community is expecting Messiah ben Joseph to be raised
from the dead at some future time by Messiah ben David, Christians believe both of these Messiahs are one and the same.

If we follow the Rabbinic teaching of Ma'aseh Avot Siman l'Banim that says,

What our fathers did, our sons also, we find striking parallels between Joseph and Yeshua that no other Messianic figure can claim for himself:

Despised and Sold

Joseph was despised by his Hebrew brothers (sons of Jacob, named Israel) and sold to Egypt for silver.

Yeshua was despised by the Jewish leaders: Pharisees, Sadducees and the Sanhedrin and sold for silver.

Considered Dead

Joseph was cut off by his brothers and considered dead by the family.

Yeshua was rejected and cut off by the Jewish leaders and was dead, lying in a tomb for three days.

Joseph was raised to the height of power and authority, second in command only to Pharaoh. As a result of Joseph's wise management of the resources under his control, many nations attached themselves to Egypt to be saved.

As Joseph states to his brothers after they buried his father Jacob (Israel), "You intended to harm me, but God intended it for good to accomplish what is now being done, the saving of many lives." *(Genesis 50:20)*

Yeshua was given all authority to rule God's Kingdom in heaven and on earth.

As a result, today 2.1 billion people claim to be Christians. Many have attached themselves to Yeshua (Jesus) to be saved and personally know Him and His Father in Heaven.

"For this reason Christ died and returned to life, so that He might be the Lord of both the dead and the living." *(Romans 14:9; see also Matthew 28:18; John 1:12, 3:35)*

Resurrected

Joseph was freed from his prison sentence to life in the palace by Pharaoh.

Yeshua was freed from death and the tomb by God.

Why Don't Rabbis Accept Yeshua As Messiah?

Even though the lives of Joseph and Yeshua parallel in so many Messianic ways, Rabbis don't believe Yeshua can be this Messiah who is the son of Joseph because they say He didn't complete the required To Do list of the Messiah

That messianic task list, which has been compiled from various Talmudic references, says that Messiah will do the following:

- **Prepare the world for the coming of Messiah, Son of David.** *(Numbers 24:17–19)*

- **Gather Israel from all corners of the world to build the Temple or at least make provisions for Messiah Son of David to enter the Temple.** *(Mishnah Torah Hilchot Melachim (Zechariah 6:13; Ezekiel 41–48)*

- **Battle with the wicked nations of the world, the enemies of Israel, especially Esau, Edom, Gog and Magog.** *(Obadiah 1:18–21; Talmud Mas. Sota 42a)*

- **Die in the battle but be resurrected (see earlier discussion)**

After Messiah ben Joseph resurrects, Messiah ben David will come to finish off the tasks appointed to the Messiah. According to Rabbis over the centuries, those tasks include the following:

- Rebuild the Temple in Jerusalem
- Restore the Jews to the Law
- Defeat the Enemies of Israel
- Defeat evil and bring about world peace

Since Yeshua (Jesus) did not complete these tasks, most Rabbis reject Him as a candidate for Messiahship.

You, like the Rabbis, may question why Yeshua didn't fulfill all the Rabbinic requirements of Messiah ben Joseph. The answer is quite simple.

First, the Rabbis who were deciding what messiah would and would not do, were against Yeshua being Messiah.

Rabbis began recording their opinions and debates about Messiah and other topics from AD 10–200 in what would become the Talmud.

The idea of the suffering Messiah ben Joseph likely started later.

In a famous second century debate titled *Dialogue with Trypho* we read a conversation about Yeshua as the Messiah.

In the dialogue, the Jewish Trypho (who is thought to be a Rabbi from the central Israeli town of Yavneh) simply cannot reconcile that a Messiah who is supposed to be glorified would become cursed on a tree, as is written in Deuteronomy 21:22–23:

"When someone is convicted of a crime punishable by death and is executed, and you hang him on a tree, his corpse must not remain all night upon the tree; you shall bury him that same day, for anyone hung on a tree is under God's curse. You must not defile the land that the Lord your God is giving you for possession."

Neither Trypho nor the Christian
Justin Martyr mentions Messiah ben
Joseph in their dialogue; instead,
Trypho looks forward to the coming of
Messiah.

This leads some scholars to believe
that the idea of this second Messiah
(ben Joseph) began to be fleshed out as
commentators added their ideas of
Messiah over the next 200–400 years.

Second, notice that the Rabbis do not
mention the defeat of sin in their
task list, which is the primary purpose
of Yeshua, even going back to the
first Messianic prophecy of a redeemer
who would crush the head of the
serpent *(Genesis 3:15).*

"And I will put enmity between thee
and the woman, and between the seed
of thy son, and the seed of her sons;
and it shall be when the sons of
the woman keep the commandments of
the law, they will be prepared to smite
thee upon thy head; but when they

forsake the commandments of the law, thou wilt be ready to wound them in their heel.

"Nevertheless for them there shall be a medicine, but for thee there will be no medicine; and they shall make a remedy for the heel in the days of the King Meshiha." *(Genesis 3:15, PJE)*

The Rabbis who wrote their task lists either didn't believe Messiah came to deal with sin, or they refused to voice this idea for fear that Yeshua could be Messiah.

Moreover, the tasks that should be included in these lists are still disputed even within Rabbinic literature.

What if the Rabbis have misinterpreted the Scriptures?

What if there is only one Messiah, who has already come once to fulfill some of the tasks and will come again to finish the job?

Yeshua: One Messiah, One Task List

When we let Scripture interpret
Scripture, one Messiah with one task
list
appears. Some of those tasks have
already been fulfilled by Yeshua
(whose
name means Salvation):

- He was the suffering servant
  *(Isaiah 52:13–53:12; 1 Peter
  2:22–25; Romans 5:6–8;
  Philippians 2:6–11)*
- He defeated sin by His death and
  resurrection *(Isaiah 53; 1 John
  3:8; Hebrews 2:14–15)*

And Yeshua will come again to
complete His final Messianic duties:

- He will defeat Israel's enemies
  (Zechariah 9–12; Revelation 20)
- He will set up the Messianic age
  *(Isaiah 2:4, 9:1–7, 11:6–9;
  Revelation 20:4–6)*

We are looking at the many duties
Messiah is to perform and prophecies
He is to fulfill, but those listed above
are His primary purposes.

Did We Miss It?

Over 100,000 Jews and two billion
non-Jews today have accepted that
Messiah has come and is coming again.
Some Jews from ancient days believe
the time for Messiah has come and
gone.
Rabbi Hillel who lived at the time of
Yeshua said, "There shall be
no Messiah for Israel because they
have already enjoyed him in the days
of Hezekiah."

Hillel thought that King Hezekiah was
the Messiah.

"May God forgive him [Hillel for
saying so]," said a Rabbi named
Joseph.

This Rabbi Joseph, a contemporary of Rav Hillel, who lived during the time of Yeshua (Jesus) stated that the Messiah is still to come and will arrive as Zechariah prophesies, riding on a donkey!

"Now, when did Hezekiah flourish? During the first Temple. Yet Zechariah prophesied that in the days of the second [Temple], proclaimed, 'Rejoice greatly, O daughter of Zion, shout, O daughter of Jerusalem, behold, thy king cometh unto thee! he is just, and having salvation, lowly, and riding upon an ass, and upon a colt the foal of an ass.'" *(Sanhedrin 99a)*

But millions more Jewish People are still looking, praying three times a day the following prayer:

"Speedily cause the offspring of your servant David to flourish, and let him be exalted by your saving power, for we wait all day long for your salvation. Blessed are you, O Lord, who causes salvation to flourish." *(Excerpt of the Amidah, or Standing Prayer)*

Why do so many Jews reject Yeshua as this Servant of David?

Part of the answer could be in the confusion that arises with two Messiahs and two task lists compiled through rigorous debate by Rabbis over many centuries.

We at Bibles For Israel believe that when we let Scripture interpret Scripture (from Genesis through Revelation), we see a picture of one task list for one Messiah that is quite different from the two task lists of the Rabbis.

Perhaps when we have finished our series searching these Messianic prophecies, more Jewish People will be "explaining and proving that the Messiah had to suffer and rise from the dead" as Rabbi Paul in the New Testament did, and say,

"This Yeshua I am proclaiming to you is the Messiah." *(Acts 17:3)*

CHAPTER FIVE

Know Your Enemy

In 1970 comedian Flip Wilson introduced Geraldine Jones into his routine. She was the wife of a preacher, and every time she would get herself in a jam because of something she did, she would say "The Devil Made Me Do It".

I was already convinced there was no such thing as "The Devil". The whole concept was preposterous. I didn't need Geraldine Jones to seal the deal for me.

In 1977 Keith Green wrote a song that seems to say it all.

His classic "No One Believes In Me Anymore" goes like this:

Still my work goes on and on
Always stronger than before
I'm gonna make it dark before the dawn
Since no one believes in me anymore
Well, now I used to have to sneak around
But now they just open their doors

You know, no one watches for my tricks
Since no one believes in me anymore
Well I'm gaining power by the hour
They're falling by the score
You know, it's getting very easy now
Since no one believes in me anymore
No one believes in me anymore
No one believes in me anymore

"Know Your Enemy" is a saying derived from Sun Tzu's *The Art of War*.

The Art of War is an ancient Chinese military treatise dating from the Late Spring and Autumn Period(771-476 BC). The work, which is attributed to the ancient Chinese military strategist Sun Tzu, is composed of 13 chapters. Each one is devoted to an aspect of warfare and how it applies to military strategy and tactics.

It's one thing if you don't know your enemy very well. But if you don't even believe there is an enemy…well, you don't even stand a fighting chance, no pun intended.

Many Jewish people struggle not only with the existence of Satan, but God as well!

2Corinthians 4:4 reads: "In whom the god of this world hath blinded the minds of them which believe not, lest the light of the glorious gospel of Messiah, who is the image of God, should shine unto them. "

We see here that those whose minds are blinded, are they who believe not; and because they believe not, their minds continue in darkness, and are proper subjects for Satan to work on; and he deepens the darkness, and increases the hardness. But who is meant by the god of this world? It is generally answered, the same who is called the prince of this world in John 16:11. But the question recurs, who is the prince of this world? and the answer to both is, Satan.

Jewish people haven't read the New Covenant, and even if they have read the Old Testament, there are only a few references where the name "HaSatan" is used. The classic is of course is in the Book of Job.

Satan Allowed to Test Job

Job 1:6 Now there was a day when the sons of God came to present themselves before the LORD, and Satan came also among them.

Job 1:7 And the LORD said unto Satan, Whence comest thou? Then Satan answered the LORD, and said, From going to and fro in the earth, and from walking up and down in it.

Job 1:8 And the LORD said unto Satan, Hast thou considered my servant Job, that *there is* none like him in the earth, a perfect and an upright man, one that feareth God, and escheweth evil?

Job 1:9 Then Satan answered the LORD, and said, Doth Job fear God for nought?

Job 1:10 Hast not thou made an hedge about him, and about his house, and about all that he hath on every side? thou hast blessed the work of his hands, and his substance is increased in the land.

Job 1:11 But put forth thine hand now, and touch all that he hath, and he will curse thee to thy face.

Job 1:12 And the LORD said unto Satan, Behold, all that he hath *is* in thy power; only upon himself put not forth thine hand. So Satan went forth from the presence of the LORD.

Satan Takes Job's Property and Children

Job 1:13 And there was a day when his sons and his daughters *were* eating and drinking wine in their eldest brother's house:

Job 1:14 And there came a messenger unto Job, and said, The oxen were plowing, and the asses feeding beside them:

Job 1:15 And the Sabeans fell *upon them,* and took them away; yea, they have slain the servants with the edge of the sword; and I only am escaped alone to tell thee.

Job 1:16 While he *was* yet speaking, there came also another, and said, The fire of God is fallen from heaven, and hath burned up the sheep, and the servants, and consumed them; and I only am escaped alone to tell thee.

Job 1:17 While he *was* yet speaking, there came also another, and said, The Chaldeans made out three bands, and fell upon the camels, and have carried them away, yea, and slain the servants with the edge of the sword; and I only am escaped alone to tell thee.

Job 1:18 While he *was* yet speaking, there came also another, and said, Thy sons and thy daughters *were* eating and drinking wine in their eldest brother's house:

Job 1:19 And, behold, there came a great wind from the wilderness, and smote the four corners of the house, and it fell upon the young men, and they are dead; and I only am escaped alone to tell thee.

Job 1:20 Then Job arose, and rent his mantle, and shaved his head, and fell down upon the ground, and worshipped,

Job 1:21 And said, Naked came I out of my mother's womb, and naked shall I return thither: the LORD gave, and the LORD hath taken away; blessed be the name of the LORD.

Job 1:22 In all this Job sinned not, nor charged God foolishly.

The dialogue continues in Chapter 2

Satan is a personal being. Concerning his creation and his fall, much is recorded in Ezekiel 28:10-19. He was the highest, most powerful creature whom God in his omnipotence and omniscience could bring into existence. He was called the anointed cherub, the cherub that covereth, and was in command of the great hosts of God.

On account of his high official position in the government of God, of his beauty, wisdom, strength, and power, he became puffed up with pride. He conceived the idea that he could match swords with the Almighty and attempted to do so. Thereupon he was cast from his high and holy position and was demoted to an inferior position in the universe. He still has great power and is indeed shrewd and evil. Though in his fallen condition, he has access to the throne of God, very evident from a perusal of the above text from Job chapter one. Like Hannibal of old, who swore eternal vengeance against Rome, Satan has sworn everlasting vengeance against God, Israel, and all who are on the Lord's side.

Of course for those Jewish people who have read the book of Job, how many believe it? Not many.

There is much written about Satan in the Talmud and Midrash.

I will include just a few examples.

As the incarnation of evil Satan is the arch-enemy of the Messiah: he is Antichrist. The *light* which was created before the world was hidden by God beneath His throne; and to the question of Satan in regard to it God answered, "*This light* is kept for him who shall bring thee to shame." At his request God showed Satan the Messiah; "and when he saw him he trembled, fell upon his face, and cried: 'Verily this is the Messiah who shall hurl me and all the princes of the angels of the peoples down even unto hell'" (Pesiḳ. R. iii. 6)

Satan was mentioned in the liturgy at an early period, as in the daily morning prayer and in the Blessing of the New Moon; and his name has naturally occurred in amulets and incantations down to the present day. Terms and phrases referring to Satan which are met with in Judæo-German must be regarded as reminiscences of the ancient popular belief in him.

The Midrash tells the tale of Satan's unsuccessful attempts to mislead, misguide and misdirect Abraham while he was en route to carry out God's order to sacrifice his son Isaac on Mount Moriah. In this Midrash, Satan tries to trick Abraham and confuse him as to the source of the sacrificial commandment. Satan is brilliant in carrying out his task and this temptation, while unsuccessful, is viewed as an important test, an integral part of Abraham's trial.

John Milton, in *Paradise Lost,* has Satan saying: "Better to reign in hell than serve in heaven." From what we see of the Satan described in the Talmud and Midrash, he is not all that interested in being of the ruling elite. He revels in his work as a tempter of mankind, a tester of the righteous. He glories in his persona as the Evil Inclination, performs brilliantly as

Angel of Death, and awaits every opportunity to function as the Accuser in the Heavenly tribunal. He is a trickster *par excellence.*

Because the Talmudic Satan is not overly intimidating, he figures in many Jewish jokes and sayings. For instance, the great Rabbi Nachman of Breslau is supposed to have said: "It was difficult for Satan alone to mislead the entire world, so he appointed rabbis in various communities." The Trickster of the Talmud and Midrash strikes again.

As humorous as that statement is, Israel and the Jewish people have suffered tremendously throughout its history because of unbelief.

According to 2Corinthians 4:4, it is Satan himself who is blinding the minds of those who don't believe, their minds continue in darkness, and as stated earlier, are proper subjects for Satan to work on.

The veil can be removed once they realize that *"we wrestle not against flesh and blood, but against principalities, against powers, against the rulers of the darkness of this world, against spiritual wickedness in high places."*

Ephesians 6:12

An atheist and agnostic for much of my life, depending on the day of the week, the realization that there really was a God came full circle for me personally, when God allowed me to see into that "unseen realm" of the spirit world, as described above in Ephesians 6:12, as well as being in the presence of a person possessed by a demon. I realized that if there were entities that were that real and terrifying, there had to be a God in heaven that was in control, and held things together. It also enabled me to recognize that there is a God who loves us and he has a plan that he is unfolding. But it also made me aware that there is a powerful supernatural enemy who opposes all that God is doing and seeks to create pain and havoc for his people.

It created in me a deep desire to search the scriptures, like the Bereans did in the Book of Acts, to find the truth through God's word. That's what we are hoping to accomplish in the hearts of your Jewish friends and associates.

CHAPTER SIX

"Mathematically Speaking"

Mathematics is the study of numbers, shapes and patterns. The word comes from the Greek , meaning "science, knowledge, or learning".

Mathematicians seek and use patterns to formulate new conjectures; they resolve the truth or falsity of conjectures by *mathematical* proof.

"Probability", one of the main branches of mathematics, is the likelihood of something happening in the future or chance of an event occurring.

As mentioned earlier, I don't enjoy jigsaw puzzles. I love math.

I was a high school math teacher for several years when I first graduated from college.

Psalm 19, the first verse states, "the heavens declare the Glory of God".

In my mind, mathematics also declare the Glory of God.

God is the necessary foundation for mathematics and therefore of every science which uses it. The argument is that mathematical laws, in order to be properly relied upon, must have attributes which indicate an origin in God. They are true everywhere (omnipresent), true always (eternal), cannot be defied or defeated (omnipotent), and are rational and have language characteristics (which makes them personal). Omnipresent, omnipotent, eternal, personal… Sounds like God. Math is an expression of the mind of God.

Following are several messianic prophesies and their "probability ratio", as well as several key prophesies from the Tenach that Jewish people probably have never read.

1. As stated earlier, sometime before 500 B.C. the prophet Daniel proclaimed that Israel's long-awaited Messiah would begin his public ministry 483 years after the issuing of a decree to restore and rebuild Jerusalem (Daniel 9:25-26). He further

predicted that the Messiah would be "cut off," killed, and that this event would take place prior to a second destruction of Jerusalem. Abundant documentation shows that these prophecies were perfectly fulfilled in the life (and crucifixion) of Yeshua of Nazareth, Jesus Christ. The decree regarding the restoration of Jerusalem was issued by Persia's King Artaxerxes to the Hebrew priest Ezra in 458 B.C., 483 years later the ministry of Yeshua began in Galilee. (Remember that due to calendar changes, the date for the start of Yeshua's ministry is set by most historians at about 26 A.D. Also note that from 1 B.C. to 1 A.D. is just one year.) Yeshua's crucifixion occurred only a few years later, and about four decades later, in 70 A.D. came the destruction of Jerusalem by Titus.

(Probability of chance fulfillment = 1 in 10^5.)*

*The estimates of probability included herein come from a group of *secular research scientists*. As an example of their method of estimation, consider their calculations for this first prophecy cited:

- Since the Messiah's ministry could conceivably begin in any one of about 5000 years, there is, then, one chance in about 5000 that his ministry could begin in 26 A.D.
- Since the Messiah is God in human form, the possibility of his being killed is considerably low, say less than one chance in 10.
- Relative to the second destruction of Jerusalem, this execution has roughly an even chance of occurring before or after that event, that is, one chance in 2.

Hence, the probability of chance fulfillment for this prophecy is 1 in 5000 x 10 x 2, which is 1 in 100,000, or 1 in 10^5. (1 in 10, with 5 zeroes added)

All of the following Messianic Prophesies follow the same formula.

2. Also mentioned earlier, in approximately 700 B.C. the prophet Micah named the tiny village of Bethlehem as the birthplace of Israel's Messiah (Micah 5:2). The fulfillment of this prophecy in the birth of Yeshua is one of the most widely known and widely celebrated facts in history.

(Probability of chance fulfillment = 1 in 10^5.)

3. In the fifth century B.C. a prophet named Zechariah declared that the Messiah would be betrayed for the price of a slave—thirty pieces of silver, according to Jewish law-and also that this money would be used to buy a burial ground for Jerusalem's poor

foreigners (Zechariah 11:12-13). Bible writers and secular historians both record thirty pieces of silver as the sum paid to Judas Iscariot for betraying Jesus, and they indicate that the money went to purchase a "potter's field," used—just as predicted—for the burial of poor aliens (Matthew 27:3-10).

(Probability of chance fulfillment = 1 in 10^{11}.)

4. Some 400 years before crucifixion was invented, both Israel's King David and the prophet Zechariah described the Messiah's death in words that perfectly depict that mode of execution. Further, they said that the body would be pierced and that none of the bones would be broken, contrary to customary procedure in cases of crucifixion (Psalm 22 and 34:20; Zechariah 12:10). Again, historians and New Testament writers confirm the fulfillment: Yeshua of Nazareth died on a Roman cross, and

his extraordinarily quick death eliminated the need for the usual breaking of bones. A spear was thrust into his side to verify that he was, indeed, dead.

(Probability of chance fulfillment = 1 in 10^{13}.)

6. For unto us a Child is born, Unto us a Son is given; and the government will be upon His shoulder. And His name will be called Wonderful, Counselor, Mighty God, Everlasting Father, Prince of Peace. Of the increase of *His* government and peace there will be no end,   upon the throne of David and over His kingdom, To order it and establish it with judgment and justice from that time forward, even forever. The zeal of the LORD of hosts will perform this .

(Probability of chance fulfillment = 1 in 10^{13}.)

This one is worth repeating.

7. Who has believed our report? And to whom has the arm of the Lord been revealed? For *He* shall grow up before Him as a tender plant, and as a root out of dry ground. *He* has no form or comeliness; and when we see *Him*, there is no beauty that we should desire Him. *He* is despised and rejected by men, a man of sorrows and acquainted with grief, and we hid, as it were, our faces from Him; *He* was despised, and we did not esteem Him. Surely *He* has born our griefs and carried our sorrows; yet we esteemed Him stricken, smitten by God, and afflicted. But *He* was wounded for our transgressions, *He* was bruised for our iniquities; The chastisement for our peace was upon Him, and by *His* stripes we are healed. All we like sheep have gone astray; We have turned, every one, to his own way; And the Lord has laid on *Him* the iniquity of us all. He was oppressed and *He* was afflicted, yet *He* opened not his mouth. *He* was taken from prison and from

judgment, and who will declare His generation? For *He* was cut off from the land of the living; for the transgressions of my people *He* was stricken. And they made *His* grave with the wicked, but with the rich at his death, because He had done no violence, nor was any deceit in his mouth. Yet it pleased the Lord to bruise *Him*; He has put Him to grief. When you make his soul an offering for sin, He shall see His seed, He shall prolong His days, and the pleasure of the Lord shall prosper in His hand. He shall see the labor of His soul, and be satisfied. By His knowledge My righteous Servant shall justify many, for *He* shall bear their iniquities. Therefore I will divide Him a portion with the great, and He shall divide the spoil with the strong, because He poured out his soul unto death, and he was numbered with the transgressors, and *He* bore the sin of many, and made intercession for the transgressors.

Contained within this chapter (Isaiah 53), written around 750 B.C., are over *20* individual prophesies. The odds are almost *incalculable* that these were all *"chance fulfillments"*. Our Rabbis would tell us that the author is speaking of "Israel". You can decide for yourself!

8. Behold, the days come, saith the Lord, that I will make a <u>New Covenant</u> with the house Israel, and with the house of Judah: Not according to the covenant that I made with their fathers in the day that I took them by the hand to bring them out of the land of Egypt; which my covenant they broke, although I was a husband to them, saith the Lord: But this shall be the covenant that I will make with the house of Israel; After those days, saith the Lord, I will put my law in their inward parts, and write it in their hearts; and I will be their God, and they shall be my people. And they shall teach no more every man his neighbor,

and every man his brother, saying, know the Lord: for they shall all know me, from the least of them unto the greatest of them, saith the Lord: for I will forgive their iniquity, and I will remember their sin no more.
(Jeremiah 31:31-34)

(Probability of chance fulfillment = 1 in 10^5.)

9. Surely, I am more brutish than any man, and have not the understanding of a man. I neither learned wisdom, nor have the knowledge of the Holy One. Who hath ascended up into heaven, and descended? Who hath gathered the wind in his fists? Who hath bound the waters in his garment? Who hath established all the ends of the earth? What is his name, and what is his Son's name, if thou knowest?   *(Proverbs 30:2-4)*

(Probability of chance fulfillment = 1 in 10^5.)

10. Yet I have set my king upon my holy hill of Zion. I will declare the decree: the Lord hath said unto me, thou art my Son; this day I have begotten thee. Ask of Me, and I shall give the nation for thine inheritance, and the ends of the earth for thy possession. Thou shall break them with a rod or iron; Thou shall dash them in pieces like a potter's vessel. Now therefore, O ye kings, be wise; Be admonished, ye judges of the earth. Serve the Lord with fear, and rejoice with trembling. Kiss the Son, lest he be angry, and ye perish from the way, when his wrath is kindled but a little. Blessed are all they that put their trust in him.   *(Psalm 2:6-12)*

(Probability of chance fulfillment = 1 in 10^5.)

Peter Stoner was Chairman of the Departments of Mathematics and Astronomy at Pasadena City College until 1953; Chairman of the science division, Westmont College, 1953–57; Professor Emeritus of Science, Westmont College; Professor Emeritus of Mathematics and Astronomy, Pasadena City College.

Stoner calculated the probability of just 8 Messianic prophecies being fulfilled in the life of Yeshua. All estimates were calculated as conservatively as possible.

Multiplying all these probabilities together produces a number (rounded off) of 1×10^{28}. Dividing this number by an estimate of the number of people who have lived since the time of these prophecies (88 billion) produces a probability of all 8 prophecies being fulfilled accidently in the life of one person. That probability is 1in 10^{17} or 1 in 100,000,000,000,000,000. That's one in one hundred quadrillion!

To illustrate that number, Stoner gave the following example: "First, blanket the entire Earth land mass with silver dollars 120 feet high. Second, specially mark one of those dollars and randomly bury it. Third, ask a person to travel the Earth and select the marked dollar, while blindfolded, from the trillions of other dollars."[1]

Bible scholars tell us that nearly 300 references to 61 specific prophecies of the Messiah were fulfilled by Yeshua. The odds against one person fulfilling that many prophecies would be beyond all mathematical possibility. It could never happen, no matter how much time was allotted. I'm going to repeat those final two lines in the hope that if you are reading it, and you don't believe that Yeshua is the Messiah, the Son of the Living God, that it will compel you to cry out to God for the Truth.

The odds against one person fulfilling that many prophecies would be beyond all mathematical possibility. It could never happen, no matter how much time was allotted!!!

EPILOGUE

Our vision in writing "The Puzzle", once again, is two-fold.

For those who have met the Messiah, and have a personal relationship with him, it contains information that can be used to challenge those who have not yet had that privilege.

Although written for the Jewish people who have not yet met their Messiah, it can be equally effective for the non-Jew as well

To my Jewish brothers and sisters, friends and family, I have been as honest and transparent as possible in presenting information that we were never made aware of growing up, or just never had the opportunity to read about. In addition, information that we were told that just wasn't truthful, I have exposed as false.

If accepting Yeshua as the Messiah is as simple as accepting "mathematical probabilities" as fact or just using common sense, well, everyone would believe in Yeshua. Even if all of the puzzle pieces were assembled, and you could see with your natural eyes the completed puzzle picture, it still has to be viewed through your spiritual eyes for it to be accepted in your heart.

There is only one way to be sure. You must ask God to reveal the truth to you.

Ask him if Yeshua is who he says he is. If your motives are pure and you are really seeking truth...you will find it.

For God so loved the world, that He gave His only begotten Son, that whoever believes in Him shall not perish, but have eternal life.

Yochanan 3:16